Gender Inequity and Poverty

By

Dr. M. Lakshmi Narasaiah
M.A., Ph.D.
Professor & Head
Department of Economics
Sri Krishnadevaraya University Post-graduate Centre
Kurnool–518 002
Andhra Pradesh (India)

DISCOVERY PUBLISHING HOUSE
NEW DELHI

First Published–2004

ISBN: 81-7141-762-0

Published by:

DISCOVERY PUBLISHING HOUSE

4831/24, Prahlad Street, Ansari Road, Darya Ganj
New Delhi–110 002 (India)
Phone: 23279245, • Fax: 91-11-23253475
e-mail: dphtemp@indiatimes.com

Printed at:

Tarun Offset Printers, Delhi-53

Preface

Understanding the differences between women and men, and how they are determined, is of key importance in understanding why a gender perspective is so important for development and the elimination of world poverty.

Differences between women and men are determined by biology, on the one hand, and society, on the other.

- Sex marks the distinction between women and men as a result of the fundamental biological, physical and genetic differences between them.
- Gender roles are set by convention and other social, economic, political and cultural forces.

The precise boundary between these factors is the subject of fierce debate. Some people believe that the only important difference is that women can bear children and men cannot. Others believe that biology determines a much wider set of characteristics, attributes, and capabilities. Whatever the case, the wide variation in the position of women in different societies around the world demonstrates that, unlike sex, gender roles are by no means fixed by nature—they are made by people, and can be renegotiated and changed.

The position of women in society is far from being of academic interest alone. It not only has fundamental consequences for the quality of life of both women and men, but also has a direct impact on a society's prosperity and well-being. The government's policy on international development recognises that gender-based inequality is a major obstacle to the escape from poverty. Studies have shown that developing countries which strive to ensure that women have equal rights have higher rates of economic growth, lower mortality rates, smaller and healthier families, and a better-educated population. Changing gender roles can make a world of difference.

The evidence also shows that gender equality is not a luxury which can only be afforded by rich countries. UN data reveals that some developing countries outperform much richer ones in the opportunities they afford women. The better performing countries are scattered throughout the world, showing that culture and religion need not be barriers to the advancement of women.

The gender gap in many countries is closing fast. Rapid progress has been made in recent decades. But in society do women fare as well as men. Women are gaining ground in health and education terms, but still have a long way to go in sharing political and economic opportunities. They continue to suffer high levels of violence and abuse, and in many countries are treated differently to men by the law. These disadvantages are not due to sex differences, but are the result of gender discrimination.

Empowerment, Equality, and Equity: What do They Mean?

Women's empowerment, gender equality and equity are key terms in debates about the changes required in the relationships between women and men.

- Empowerment means individuals acquiring the power to think and act freely, exercise choice, and to fulfil their potential as full and equal members of society.
- Equality means that women should have the same rights and entitlements as men to human, social, economic and cultural development, and equal voice in civil and political life. It does not men that everyone should be the same, or that the benefits of development should be shared in exactly equal proportions by everyone. This would be neither feasible nor desirable, and would not be consistent with the notion of empowerment, which upholds everyone's right to determine their own future and the lifestyle of their choice.

Dr. M. Lakshmi Narasaiah

Contents

Preface

1. Sex and Gender: *A World of Difference* 1
2. Gender–Based Violence 4
3. Do Men Matter? New Horizons in Gender and Development 7
4. One Battle after Another 10
5. For a Fair Sharing of Time 14
6. Safe Motherhood is a Human Rights Issue 18
7. Action for Safe Motherhood 21
8. What is Known about Reducing Maternal Mortality? 25
9. Women in Politics 27
10. Fighting for Equality on All Fronts 31
11. Equal Opportunities for Women in the Community 36
12. Lightening the Load for Women 39
13. Women and Poverty 42
14. Women in Authority: *The Ideal and the Reality* 45
15. Promotion of Women 48
16. Empowerment for Women? 52
17. Population Growth and Women's Role in India 56
18. No Progress without a Secular Society 61
19. On the Way to Commercial Microcredits 63

20. Measuring Population's Inpact 71
21. All Human Rights for All 74
22. The Coming Water Crisis 76
23. Using Economics to Advantage 79
24. Law and Social Justice 82
25. AIDS and the Responsibility of the Media 85
26. Pollution for Export 88
27. Human Rights–The Road to Progress and Peace 92
28. Energy: *A Fair Deal for All* 95
29. Food for the Billions 100
30. Food Production 103
31. Taking Poverty to Heart 107
32. Land Tunure: *Securing Land for the Urban Poor* 111
Bibliography 115
Index 125

Sex and Gender

A World of Difference

Understanding the differences between women and men, and how they are determined, is of key importance in understanding why a gender perspective is so important for development and the elimination of world poverty.

Differences between women and men are determined by biology, on the one hand, and society, on the other.

- Sex marks the distinction between women and men as a result of the fundamental biological, physical and genetic differences between them.
- Gender roles are set by convention and other social, economic, political and cultural forces.

The precise boundary between these factors is the subject of fierce debate. Some people believe that the only important difference is that women can bear children and men cannot. Others believe that biology determines a much wider set of characteristics, attributes, and capabilities. Whatever the case, the wide variation in the position of women in different societies around the world demonstrates that, unlike sex, gender roles are by no means fixed by nature –they are made by people, and can be renegotiated and changed.

The position of women in society is far from being of academic interest alone. It not only has fundamental consequences for the quality of life of both women and men, but also has a direct impact on a society's prosperity and well-being. The government's policy on international development recognises that gender-based inequality is a major obstacle to the escape from poverty. Studies have shown that developing countries which strive to ensure that women have equal rights have higher rates of economic growth, lower mortality rates, smaller and healthier families, and a better-educated population. Changing gender roles can make a world of difference.

The evidence also shows that gender equality is not a luxury which can only be afforded by rich countries. UN data reveals that some developing countries outperform much richer ones in the opportunities they afford women. The better performing countries are scattered throughout the world, showing that culture and religion need not be barriers to the advancement of women.

The gender gap in many countries is closing fast. Rapid progress has been made in recent decades. But in no society do women fare as well as men. Women are gaining ground in health and education terms, but still have a long way to go in sharing political and economic opportunities. They continue to suffer high levels of violence and abuse, and in many countries are treated differently to men by the law. These disadvantages are not due to sex differences, but are the result of gender discrimination.

Empowerment, Equality, and Equity: What do They Mean?

Women's empowerment, gender equality and equity are key terms in debates about the changes required in the relationships between women and men.

- Empowerment means individuals acquiring the power to think and act freely, exercise choice, and to fulfil their potential as full and equal members of society.
- Equality means that women should have the same rights and entitlements as men to human, social, economic and cultural development, and equal voice in civil and political life. It does not mean that

everyone should be the same, or that the benefits of development should be shared in exactly equal proportions by everyone. This would be neither feasible nor desirable, and would not be consistent with the notion of empowerment, which upholds everyone's right to determine their own future and the lifestyle of their choice.

- Equity means that the exercise of these rights should lead to outcomes which are fair and just, and which enable women to have the same power as men to define and pursue the objectives of development and shape societies of the future.

The difference between equality and equity is important because it underlines the rights of women to define the objectives of development for themselves, and to seek outcomes which are not necessarily identical to those sought or enjoyed by men. Women have the right to pursue development paths which reflect their own needs and aspirations.

Upholding these rights is in the interests of men as well as women, because of the wider social and economic benefits brought by gender equality. Because of the universal disadvantages experienced by women, their empowerment is crucial to the achievement of equality and equity, the elimination of poverty and a better world for all.

2

Gender-Based Violence

Around the world at least one woman in every three has been beaten, coerced into sex, or otherwise abused in her lifetime. Most often the abuser is a member of her own family. Increasingly, gender-based violence is recognised as a major public health concern and a violation of human rights.

The effects of violence can be devastating to a woman's reproductive health as well as to other aspects of her physical and mental well-being. In addition to causing injury, violence increases women's long-term risk of a number of other health problems, including chronic pain, physical disability, drug and alcohol abuse, and depression. Women with a history of physical or sexual abuse are also at increased risk for unintended pregnancy, sexually transmitted infections, and adverse pregnancy outcomes. Yet victims of violence who seek care from health professionals often have needs that providers do not recognize, do not ask about, and do not know how to address.

What is Gender-Based Violence?

Violence against women and girls includes physical, sexual, psychological and economic abuse. It is often known as "gender-based" evidence because it evolved in part from women's subordinate status in society. Many cultures have beliefs, norms, and social institutions that legitimize and therefore perpetuate violence against women. The same acts that would be punished if directed at an employer, a neighbour, or an acquaintance often go unchallenged when men direct them at women, especially within the family.

Two of the most common forms of violence against women are abuse by intimate male partners and coerced sex, whether it takes place in childhood, adolescence, or adulthood. Intimate partner abuse—also known as domestic violence, wife-beating, and battering—is almost always accompanied by psychological abuse and in one-quarter to one-half of cases by forced sex as well. The majority of women who are abused by their partners are abused many times. In fact, an atmosphere of terror often permeates abusive relationships.

How Health Care Providers Can Help

Health care providers can do much to help their clients who are victims of gender-based violence. Yet providers often miss opportunities to help by being unaware, indifferent, or judgemental. With training and support from health care systems, providers can do more to respond to the physical, emotional, and security needs of abused women and girls.

First, health care providers can learn how to ask women about violence in ways that their clients find helpful. They can given women empathy and support. They can provide medical treatment, offer counseling, document injuries, and refer their clients to legal assistance and support services.

Family planning and other reproductive health care providers have a particular responsibility to help because.

- Abuse has a major—although little recognized—impact on women's reproductive health and sexual well-being;
- Providers cannot do their jobs well unless they understand how violence and powerlessness affect women's reproductive health and decision-making ability.
- Reproductive health care providers are strategically placed to help identify victims of violence and connect them with other community support services.

Providers can reassure women that violence is unacceptable and that no woman deserves to be beaten, sexually abused, or made to suffer emotionally.

Societal Responses

Health workers alone cannot transform the cultural, social, and legal environment that gives rise to and condones widespread violence against women. Ending physical and sexual violence requires a long-term commitment and strategies involving all parts of society. Many governments have committed themselves to overcoming violence against women by passing and enforcing laws that ensure women's legal rights and punish abusers. In addition, community-based strategies can focus on empowering women, reaching out to men, and changing the beliefs and attitudes that permit abusive behaviour. Only when women gain their place as equal members of society will violence against women no longer be an invisible norm but, instead, a shocking aberration.

3

Do Men Matter?

New Horizons in Gender and Development

Why do men not feature more in gender and development policy? The shift in emphasis from Women in Development (WID) to Gender and Development (GAD), from enumerating and redressing women's disadvantages to analysing the social relationships between men and women, has not led to a recognition within policy of the need to understand the position of women and men. Is there a need for an explicit focus on men in GAD?

With a few notable exceptions, men are rarely explicity mentioned in gender policy documents. Where men do appear, they are generally seen as obstacles to women's development; men must surrender their positions of dominance for women to become empowered. The superiority of women as hard working, reliable, trustworthy, socially responsible, caring and co-operative is often asserted, whilst men on the other hand are frequently portrayed as lazy, violent, promiscuous and irresponsible drunkards.

Why, then, focus on men? Emerging critiques of policy argue for special attention to be paid to men and masculinities in development as follows:

Gender is Relational

It concerns the relationships between men and women which are subject to negotiation in private and public spheres. To focus on women only is inadequate; a better understanding of men's perceptions and positions and the scope for changing these, is essential. Exploring masculinities includes focusing on socially constructed 'ways of being a man rather than simply on their physical and sexual attributes. Biological essentialism is rejected in favour of an analysis of the social context within gendered roles and relations are formed.

Equality and Social Justice

Gender concerns should not simply be viewed as instrumental in securing a more effective delivery of development. Instead, this critique recognises that men as well as women may be disadvantagous by social and economic structures and that they both have the right to live free from poverty and repression. Empowerment processes should also enable women and men to be liberated from the confines of gender stereotyped roles.

Gendered Vulnerabilities

Evident from several studies suggests that while women in general may face greater social and economic disadvantages, men are not always the winners and that generalising about their situation risks overlooking gender-specific inequities and vulnerabilities, such as the damaging health effects of certain 'masculine' labour roles of social practices.

Crisis of Masculinity

It is suggested that changes in the economy, social structures, and household composition are resulting in crises of masculinity in many parts of the world. The 'demasculinising' effects of poverty and of economic and social change may be eroding men's traditional roles as providers and limiting the availability of alternative, meaningful roles for men in families and communities. Men may consequently seek affirmation of their masculinity in other ways, through irresponsible sexual behaviour or domestic violence for example.

Strategic Gendered Partnerships

There is a strong argument that if gender equitable changes are to be achieved in households, communities and organisations, then surely men are needed as allies and partners? This links to concerns about the need to mainstream gender issues in development policy to ensure that they are not sidelined or under-funded as 'women's issues'.

Men and masculinities is a relatively new era in gender and development. Ideas concerning policy implications are in their infancy. How can research, policy, and training contribute to the debate and complete the shift from WID to GAD so that the situation of women and men is better understood? Suggestions include:

- investigating the changing roles, needs and identities of men over life courses
- researching men's roles in families, the reproduction of gender inequities through work, and men's specific health vulnerabilities.
- tracking and monitoring changes in gender relationships over time, in different cultural contexts, in association with programmes and policies
- developing positive role models for men and boys influencing mass media images, establishing activities in schools, NGOs, religious and youth groups.
- ensuring that legal frameworks support gender equity, through regulating working hours, parental leave provision, improved maintenance and inheritance law for example.
- improving gender training within development organisations to focus on gender and not women alone: for example by increasing the number of male gender trainers and improving gender analysis frameworks.

4

One Battle after Another

Women fought for their rights throughout the twentieth century. In the past several decades, their struggle has truly become global, but all is far from won. We often hear that this will be the century of women, in light of the tremendous strides that have been made in the past thirty years or so. Although it is far too soon to confirm this prediction, it can safely be asserted that the twentieth century was marked by their struggle to leave the home, where they were confined by the ancestral division of roles along gender lines. Around the world, women have campaigned to win the rights they have been denied and to build, side-by-side with men, the future of the planet.

True, such struggles had already been waged in the past, although they were deliberately shunned in official historical accounts. But the brief revolts of this special "minority", which accounts for over half of humanity, did not change the place of women in their societies. They may have ruled the roost, sometimes enjoying undeniable respect, but nevertheless they were still born to serve men and bring their husbands' descendants into the world.

Education: Their First Struggle

Yet, at the start of the twentieth century, the traditional distribution of roles, seemingly legitimised by every religion and frozen in a "natural" order, began to crumble under the two-pronged assault of modernisation and women's struggle for their collective emancipation. They waged many battles to gradually obtain, despite set-backs, a change in their status—which is still far from achieved.

The first struggle of the twentieth century was for education. In 1861, a young woman graduated in finance with a baccalaureate, a high school leaving examination, for the first time. In 1900, the first female university was founded in Japan. The same year, girls won the right to secondary education in Egypt and the first girls' school opened in Tunisia. Young women who could make the most of these new educational opportunities, not only to became better household managers and good educators for their children, as the main discourse of the period suggests, but also to do something unprecedented: to enter the forbidden spheres of public life, to exercise citizenship and to participate in politics. Throughout the twentieth century, women waged a battle on two fronts: by fighting for their own rights and taking part in the major social, political emancipation movements.

The earliest feminist movements, which first appeared in the West in the late nineteenth century, focused on workplace and civil rights issues. Industry needed women's labour, which was underpaid in comparison with that of their male counterparts. 'Equal pay for equal work!' demanded American and European women, who began setting up their own trade unions and organizing strikes. They made unquestionable strides, but after more than one century of struggle, most women around the world still earn less pay for equal work.

The Right to Vote

The second objective of the twentieth century's pioneers was participation in public life, which hinged first and foremost on having the right to vote. The struggle was long and sometimes violent, as shown by the British "suffragettes" who demonstrated in the streets or Chinese women who made their demands heard by invading their country's new parliament in 1912. Everywhere, the fierce resistance of the political world progressively yielded to determined women's movements.

Control Over Their Own Bodies

For a while, women's rights movements took a back seat to the Second World War and liberation struggles in the European colonies. The fight against fascism and, after 1945, colonialism, mobilized all their energy. Women distinguished themselves in these struggles, but that did not suffice to establish their rights as a gender. However, the world continued to change. With independence, many women in the South won access to schooling, salaried employment and, in a few exceptional cases, the closed world of politics. In Western countries, the post-war period saw them enter the work force on a massive scale. The gap between social reality and the discriminatory laws defended by exclusively male power structures grew wider.

In the West, the second generation of feminists emerged in the wake of the libertarian movements of 1968. Picking up where their elders left off, they broadened the scope of their demands, for late-twentieth century feminists no longer aspired to the right to be "just like men". Challenging the claim of the "White male" to represent university, their goal was to achieve equality while remaining distinct as women. The women's liberation movement that first emerged in the American middle-class claimed the right to control one's own body. Feminists fought for contraception and abortion rights in many countries where one or both were against the law, and for autonomy and equality within the couple. "The personal is political", proclaimed women inspired by Marxism and psychoanalysis. "Workers of the World, who washes your socks?" chanted demonstrators in the streets of Paris in the 1970s. In France, the Veil law legalizing abortion unleashed emotional debate in 1974.

Many Third World women could not identify with the struggles being waged in the West and insisted on leading their own battles at their own pace. However, these Western feminist movements breathed new life into the cause. Recognizing the changes and proclaiming their intention to accelerate them, the United Nations declared 1975 "International Women's Year" and organized the first international women's conference in Mexico City.

Already proclaimed in the Universal Declaration of Human Rights in 1948, sexual equality was reasserted in 1929 by the Convention on the Abolition of All Forms of Discrimination Against Women, which became a precious emancipation tool in the North as well as the South. At UN conferences in Copenhagen in 1980, Nairobi in 1985 and Beijing in 1995, women from both hemispheres found common ground, demanding the right to "have a child if I want it, when I want it," rejecting Malthusian principles and claiming their place in political bodies that until then had decided the world's future without them, struggling against religious fundamentalism that jeopardizes their modest gains.

Misogyny of the Political Class

Of course, the struggle of Kuwaiti women against those who have denied that the right to vote or Indian women against the forced abortion of female foetuses is not the same as American women's battle against their own fundamentalists or Fresh women's campaign against the misogyny take different approaches depending on the continent and do not necessarily have the same priorities, but the struggle has nonetheless become global during the past several decades. In the last twenty-five years, women have gradually increased their presence in public life, although it can hardly be said that the doors are wide open for them. From Africa to Asia, women's organizations have multiplied and acquired experience.

But their victories remain incomplete and the future is uncertain. From the nightmare of Afghan women to the ways in which equality is resisted in the so-called most advanced countries, the obstacles show that there is still a long way to go. Will women see the end of the struggle in this century that has just begun, the one which supposedly belongs to them?

5

For a Fair Sharing of Time

Women may have entered public life on a massive scale, but they are still on their own when it comes to running the household. A new balance must be struck if there is to be genuine democracy. At the drawn of the 21st century, states and the international community can no longer refute the fact that humanity is made up of two sexes, not just one. This discovery, a precious legacy of the century that just closed, has brought women's existence into the limelight. One of the great democratic challenges for societies over the next century will be to mature so that both sexes are able to live their lives on an equal footing, with all their differences, contrasting history and culture, but also with equal rights and responsibilities.

Women's rise to power and their participation in politics are the vital signs of a healthy democracy. If only this vision that emerged from the 1995 Beijing Women's Conference could spread worldwide! One can call it a radicalisation of democracy. When women take part in the public arena, contributing to the ongoing, shared effort to shape better ways of living together, a qualitative leap occurs. Their participation fills a gap which has until now prevented the emergence of a truly democratic culture.

Archaic Attitudes

But attitudes are not the only obstacle to women's ambitions. The structure of society and the way men and women run their daily lives are other stumbling blocks. The

Inter-American Development Bank has had the good idea of giving the Institute for Cultural Action, an NGO in Rio de Janeiro, the task of setting up a pilot programme to train women for positions of political and social power. Participants include trade union and NGO leaders, key figures from the black and indigenous communities, company executives, civil servants and policymakers.

These women of different ages, educational backgrounds and ethnic origins are all aware of one fact: they are paying a very high price for a social contract that was negotiated when women were in a position of weakness, and agree that this has to change.

Re-mapping the Division Between Public and Private Life

In Rio de Janeiro revealed that there is an urgent need to reorganize the use of time, to strike a new balance between responsibilities and to re-map the division between public and private life. Household tasks must be recognised as time consuming, socially and economically vital and a serious check on women's ambitions.

Women in positions of power must constantly prove that they can behave like men. They keep quiet about having to look after children, run a household and care for elderly parents. Bringing those issues out into the open would mean admitting "flaws" that men do not have, for the simple reason that they delegate such work to their wives.

By drawing a veil of silence over their home life as if it were something illicit, women are allowing a basic fact to be hidden: the world of work relies on a domestic zone run by them. Women have changed, but the world of work has not and they are reaching the point of exhaustion. Filled with a deep sense of injustice, they are asking themselves: "Where did I go wrong?"

Understanding that humanity is composed of two different but equal sexes has several implications. Society must redefine itself because women are turning up in public carrying children in their arms and breast-feeding them, and because they have their own awareness and language that come from life experiences which are different from those of men.

An Untenable Double Burden

Articulating issues affecting public and private life is complicated, but that does not mean the equation is impossible of that the problems they raise should be brushed aside especially since the two worlds of public and private life are intertwined and mutually supportive. The balance between the two has now been upset. Women have entered public life on a massive scale, but the organization of home life how time is used and who is responsible for what tasks is till the same, as if nothing had changed. And yet such a world, where women are expected to soldier on just as before, "simply" adding to their lives' experiences hitherto reserved to men, is called egalitarian.

That misunderstanding is fueled by an age-old tradition of dismissing the world of women, even by women themselves. Because society does not consider what they do in the home as having any major social significance, it fails to add this part of their lives to the other side of the equation.

This is why the massive migration of women from the home to the public arena is occurring without societies having to think seriously about how and by whom domestic work will be done in the future (and which women still do, but at what cost!). The double burden, resulting from an outdated social contract, is putting women under mounting pressure by speeding up their lives to an untenable pace. We are facing a social problem that society as a whole must solve and not, as many think, a problem that women must settle by working even harder.

As new area of power open up to women, both sexes must take a fresh look at how they use time. Re-arranging it is a challenge to society's imagination. But has this necessity sunk into the minds of decision-makers? I do not think so. This poses a major problem because it is a missing building block in the construction of our democracies.

The everyday work is proof of this. Women must put these issues on the political and economic agenda, thereby contributing to a more radical definition of democracy. Feminism's new demand for a different sharing of time also opens a debate that goes beyond the interests of women alone. In the final analysis, time and its constants define the limits of our own lives and the range of choices we make, in accordance with the meaning we give to our own existence.

The equality equation is increasingly complex. It is not enough to wipe out the last traces of discrimination in public life. A new definition of equality will emerge when both sexes start sharing responsibility in the private realm. Otherwise, the issue will be distorted and women will lose all chance of succeeding in public life.

6

Safe Motherhood is a Human Rights Issue

The death of a woman during pregnancy or childbirth is not only a health issue but also a matter of social injustice. Of the human rights currently acknowledged in national constitutions and in regional and international human rights treaties, many can be applied to safe motherhood. Many such treaties and conventions are based on the 1948 Declaration of Human Rights; (1) they include the Convention on the Elimination of All Forms of Discrimination against Women, (2) the Convention on the Rights of the Child, (3) the European Convention for the Protection of Human Rights and Fundamental Freedoms, (4) the American Convention on Human Rights, (5) and the African Charter on Human and Peoples' Rights (6).

Human rights of relevance to safe motherhood can be grouped into the following four principal categories:

- ❒ **Rights relating to life, liberty and security of the person,** which require governments to ensure both access to appropriate health care during pregnancy and childbirth, and women's rights to decide whether, when, and how often to bear children. Governments must therefore address factors within the economic, legal, social, and health systems that deny women these fundamental rights.
- ❒ **Rights relating to the foundation of families and of family life,** which require governments to

provide access to health services and other facilities that women need to establish families and to enjoy life within a family.

- **Rights relating to health care and the benefits of scientific progress, including health information and education,** which require governments to provide access to good sexual and reproductive health care with appropriate referral systems. The measures needed to ensure safe motherhood can be provided through primary health care irrespective of a country's level of economic development. Central to these rights is information on a range of reproductive health issues, including family planning, abortion, and sex education.

- **Rights relating to equality and non-discrimination,** which require governments to provide access to services such as education and health care without discriminatory grounds such as sex, marital status, age, and socio-economic class. Discriminatory policies include requirements for a women to obtain the consent of her husband for particular health care interventions, requirements for parental authorization which have a differential impact on girls, and laws that criminalize medical procedures that only women need. Governments are in violation of their obligations when they fail to implement laws that effectively protect women's interests or to allocate health resources to meet women's particular need for safe pregnancy and childbirth.

The actions that governments need to take to promote safe motherhood as a human right fall into three groups:

- Reform of laws that prevent women from attaining the highest possible levels of health and nutrition needed for safe pregnancy and childbirth and that inhibit access to reproductive health information and services such as laws requiring women in need of health care to seek the authorization of husbands or other family members first.

- Implemention of laws that foster women's rights to good health and nutrition and that protect women's health interests such as laws that prohibit child marriage, female genital mutilation, rape, and sexual abuse. Every effort should be made to implement laws that encourage the healthy timing of births, such as those that support the education of girls, set a minimum age for marriage, and ensure women's access to essential health care.

- Application of human rights in national legislation and policy to advance safe motherhood.

7

Action for Safe Motherhood

Countries very enormously in terms of the situations and challenges they face and their capacity to address these. However, experience from around the world over the past decade has demonstrated that a number of features are common to successful efforts to address maternal mortality. Reducing maternal mortality requires coordinated, long-term efforts. Actions are needed within families and communities, in society as a whole, in health systems, and at the level of national legislation and policy. Further, interactions among the interventions in these areas are critical to reducing maternal mortality and to building and supporting momentum for change.

Legislative and Policy Actions

Changes in legislation and policy are essential to ensure safe motherhood. Long-term political commitment is an essential prerequisite. When decision-makers at the highest levels are resolved to address maternal mortality, the resources needed will be mobilized and the essential policy decisions will be taken. Without this level of commitment over the long term, projects cannot become programmes and activities cannot be sustained.

A supportive social, economic, and legislative environment allows women to overcome the various obstacles that limit their access to health care, such as distance from their homes to appropriate health facilities, lack of transport and, more critically, financial and social barriers. Proper maternal health care is limited when women have to pay for services and essential drugs, and when they must bear substantial hidden costs such as time lost for housework, paid employment, food production, and child care. Legislation that supports women's access to care must be formulated to permit health workers at the periphery of the health system to perform specific life-saving functions. Failing this, only highly skilled health professionals, based largely in urban centres, can provide such care, and only women with sufficient money and the means to reach such centres can benefit from it.

With these objectives, careful review of national laws and policies is necessary, particularly in the following areas:

- **Family planning:** Statutes that restrict women's access to family planning services (e.g. by requiring that a woman be married or that she should have her husband's approval) should be repealed. Policies must ensure that all couples and individuals have access to good-quality, voluntary, client-oriented, and confidential family planning information and to services that offer a wide choice of effective contraceptive methods. Policies should address regulatory, social, economic, and cultural factors that limit women's control over sexuality and reproduction, in order that pregnancies that are too early, too late, or too frequent may be avoided.

- **Adolescents and children:** Polices and programmes should encourage later marriage and childbearing and an expansion of the economic and educational opportunities for girls and women. Promotion of good nutrition in childhood and adolescence, as well as supplementation if necessary during pregnancy, provides protection for both women and their future children. Policies should also enable adolescents to take responsibility for and protect their sexual and reproductive health, and facilitate their access to health information and services. All children, before they reach the age at which they become sexually active, need to be taught the risks of unprotected sex and helped to develop the skills needed to protect themselves from sexual coercion.

- **Barriers to access:** Assigning health workers trained in midwifery to village-based health facilities can help overcome problems of distance and transport. Health workers should also be trained to deal sympathetically with women patients. Policies should support the provision of services at minimum cost; at the same time, health workers should have job security, be paid adequate wages, and be provided with sufficient supplies to do their jobs. Policies that will increase women's decision-making power, particularly in regard to their own health, are also essential.

- **Regulation of practice:** Protocols and statutes aimed at providing both routine maternal care and referral facilities for obstetric complications at each level of the health system need to be developed. Responsibilities at each level for supervision, deployment of health care personnel, remuneration, and reporting procedures must be defined nationally. Development and promotion of education and training curricula are important, as is the setting of national norms and standards to govern the selection of trainees, trainers, and supervisors.

- **Delegation of authority:** Services should be decentralized so that facilities are available as close to people's homes as possible. Adequate supplies and equipment and trained staff should be available in all health facilities, particularly in rural and remote areas, together with written policies and protocols to guide service provision and to allow certain functions to be delegated to personnel at lower levels (when appropriately trained).

- **Abortion:** Availability of services for management of abortion complications and post-abortion care should be ensured by appropriate legislation. Where abortion is not prohibited by law, facilities for the safe termination of pregnancy should be made available. National policy can discourage unsafe abortion practices by promoting protection against unwanted pregnancy, and national health campaigns to publicize the risks of unsafe abortion and the need to recognize and seek treatment for abortion complications.

8

What is Known about Reducing Maternal Mortality?

Historical records demonstrate the significant improvements that can be achieved when key interventions are in place. Reductions in maternal mortality took place in Sweden during the 1800s, for example, as a result of a national policy favoring professional midwifery care for all births, coupled with establishment of standards for quality of care. By the beginning of the 20th century, maternal mortality in Sweden was the lowest around 230 per 1,00,000 live births compared with over 500 per 1,00,000 in the mid-1880s. In Denmark, Japan, Netherlands, and Norway, similar strategies produced comparable results. In England and Wales, significant reductions in maternal mortality were not apparent until the 1930s; at the national level, political commitment to the strategy was achieved only slowly and the introduction of professional midwifery was correspondingly delayed. In every case however, the key to these improvements was the institution of fully professional maternity care.

In the USA, where strategy focused on hospital delivery by doctors, maternal mortality remained high because it proved difficult to establish adequate regulatory frameworks and mechanisms to ensure quality of care. In 1930, the maternal mortality ratio in the USA was still 700 per 1,00,000 live births compared with 430 in England and Wales.

More recently, India witnessed significant reductions in maternal mortality in a relatively short period. From a level of over 1,500 per 1,00,000 live births in 1940-1945, maternal mortality fell to 555 per 1,00,000 in 1950-1955, 239 per 1,00,000 within 10 years, and 95 per 1,00,000 by 1980. The figure is now 30 per 1,00,000. These improvements followed the introduction of a system health facilities around the country allied to an expansion of midwifery skills and the spread of family planning. During the 1950s most births in India took place at home with the assistance of untrained birth attendants. By the end of the 1980s over 85 per cent of all births were attended by trained personnel.

Similar evidence of the effectiveness of health care interventions is available form China, Cuba, and Malaysia. These countries established community-based maternal health care systems comprising prenatal, delivery, and postpartum care and a system of referral to a higher level of care in the event of obstetric complications.

What these examples clearly demonstrate is that a country' overall economic wealth is not in itself the most important determinant of maternal mortality. There are numerous other examples of countries with modest levels of GNP which have achieved low maternal mortality.

9

Women in Politics

The participation of women in political life is today on the agendas of most political parties in India. However, attempts to translate this goal into concrete reality have had limited success. A basic reason for this is the lack of conceptual clarity about the genuine commitment to the issue. For any such endeavour to be successful, it must be recognised that the equal participation of women and men in decision-making in all spheres is a prerequisite for effective democracy.

Participation means more than female membership in political parties, female voter turnout in elections or a token female presence in political bodies. Participation must be meaningful and effective, and must include representation in the political arena. This includes not only formal or higher level decision-making forums, but also other political units: the family, community groups, associations, trade unions and local bodies. These are crucial areas for intervention within which women can easily understand the issues and play an effective role.

The identification of barriers to women's political participation is obviously a prerequisite for overcoming them, but the visible barriers do not necessarily reflect the entire situation, and are often merely indicative of more deep-rooted problems. Governments tend to address the issue by devising measures capable of showing quick results. But tackling visible barriers without addressing their root causes results at best in temporary success.

Overcoming the barriers means not only eliminating them but also ensuring women's participation through other means. Affirmative action measures should not be perceived as privileges or concessions, but as interim measures to reverse existing imbalances, until such time as genuine equality and parity is achieved.

India must review its policies, constitution and legislation to see whether these have been discriminatory towards women, or have been ineffective in promoting women's rights. Since the issue of women's participation cannot be addressed in isolation, one must identify and assess factors affecting the development of a democratic culture or the recognition of human rights concerns. These factors include the country's political history, its socio-cultural, ethnic and religious diversity, the impact of traditional, customary, feudal and tribal laws, and the use of religious interpretations regarding women's rights.

One must review the prevalent general situation of women. While inequalities and imbalances exist in all places some have stronger patriarchal structures wherein gender roles are more rigidly assigned. It is particularly important to assess women's political participation, including political rights, participation in election process and political parties, representation in legislative bodies and local councils, women in the civil service and in trade unions, and women's groups and lobbies.

Barriers to women's political participation can be legal, social, financial or political. In addition to identifying such barriers, it is useful to assess initiatives taken by governments and non-governmental organisations (NGOs), to evaluate successes and failures, identify the reasons and make modifications.

Based on the above, appropriate multi-pronged strategies and actions must be devised. It is important to develop a clear policy articulating the effective involving of women in the formulation of laws and policies which govern their lives.

Measures must be taken to ensure the principle of equality as a fundamental right. National legislation must be amended or repealed to remove any discriminatory provision. Positive legislation must be introduced to promote or protect affirmative action measures. The language of the law must clearly address itself to men and women, changing the practice of using the legal 'he' to include 'she'.

Research must be undertaken to cover information gaps. Monitoring mechanisms, guidelines and indicators must be devised and a process of periodic data collection established, to assess changing trends. Documentation and analysis of innovative initiatives must be ongoing, to help in devising and modifying strategies.

Women's human rights and power sharing issues must be integrated in all training programmes of government, semi-government and autonomous institutions. Key personnel involved in decision-making and implementation need to be made sensitive to gender issues. Political education and training programmes for women are needed at the community level, for NGOs and community-based organisations, communicators, development workers and media personnel, etc.

Campaigns to change attitudes and social norms and project a positive image of women can be run through educational efforts and the media, and public discussions and debates. A clear stand should be taken against any misrepresentation of religion which stands in the way of women's equality and political participation.

Workshops and seminars should promote closer interaction between women in NGOs, advocacy and research groups, government departments, political leadership, trade unions, workers' associations and the media.

A minimum quota should be established for women in all sectors and grades of the civil service, including government, semi-government and autonomous orgnisations. A minimum percentage of key advisory positions, directorships, etc, should be reserved for women. Advertisements for government jobs should specifically state women's eligibility.

Electoral rolls should be systematically updated to include all eligible women. Education should be provided on electoral rights, political parties, election issues and concrete ways of holding candidates and political parties accountable. Political parties should publish their positions on women's rights issues, and encourage women to vote on issues that concern them. Constitutions of political parties should exclude provisions which condone or justify discrimination.

An adequate minimum representation of women in legislative bodies and local councils can be ensured by reserving seats through such means as putting women's names in priority positions on lists, providing financial support to female candidates, and making legal provisions that only those parties which give certain minimum number of tickets to women are eligible to contest elections.

A government ministry with the requisite authority should be designated as a focal point for devising policy, ensuring implementation and coordinating with other ministries and agencies.

An autonomous Permanent Commission on the Status of Women should be set up to function as a thinktank on women's issues, to commission policy research and to review, recommend and monitor the implementation of policies and programmes in the field of development, rights and political participation. The Commission should comprise government representatives, NGOs, human rights organisations and experts in different areas.

A judicial authority should expedite women's human rights cases; this could take the form of a human rights bench, a tribunal or an equality ombudsman. These are only some of the basic principles and guidelines that can be adopted. Ultimately, however, no strategy can be effective unless it is also backed by the requisite political will and impetus.

Fighting for Equality on All Fronts

In the wake of unemployment, global competition and deregulation, more and more women are joining an unforgiving job market. Are they in a position to exercise force against the discrimination they experience, and can they impose equality of opportunity? To change things, women need to enter into combat on several fronts.

"For a long time, companies considered publicity to be a luxury and, in difficult times, the `advertising and communications' budget was always the first to be slashed. Today, employers have become more aware that publicity has become a trump card in their strategy. Why can't a similar awareness become possible on the subject of women's employment?"

Financial problems and an evolution of mentality are the two core themes discussed in this paper on the Equality of Women in the world of work.

A Dual Observation

It is of a twofold general observation: women are more increasingly joining the ranks of the active population: however, this trend is not matched by a parallel improvement in the quality of jobs to which they have access.

It is foreseen that women's rate of participation will be close to that of men by the year 2010. In developing countries, the rate of women's activity is only 31 per cent on average, but this figure does not take into account the very large female participation in the informal sector and in agriculture. Thus, for example, in India, the adoption of a more general definition of "economic activity" pushed the participation of women from 13 to 88 per cent.

Women remained constrained in a relatively limited number of "feminine" sectors and occupations which are generally less well-paid and are less prestigious. During the last decade, however, an upward trend has emerged and more women are acceding to management and administrative posts and to specialized and technical professions. Moreover, an increasing number of women are setting up their own businesses. It can be noted, nonetheless, that very few salaried women are able to reach the higher echelons of responsibility due to the well-known "glass ceiling".

Among other disturbing observations is the increase in part-time work, which is especially prevalent among women with young children; other types of atypical work include temporary and occasional jobs, homework and subcontracting. Part-time workers are often young women who are less educated and less qualified than the average, which makes them more vulnerable. In Africa, in Asia and in Latin America, women are being called upon more and more to find work in the informal sector.

Even though some progress has been made in the area of wages, women's salaries are still between one-half and 80 per cent of those earned by men. Women's work is underestimated in most of the societies, and their income does not match their contribution to the economy. The difference in wages cannot be attributed to conditions of work alone. In the United States, in 1994 a women in her twenties was likely to be earning 90 per cent of the rate of salary of her male counterpart.

Financial Problems

Financial problems and mentality issues emerged as two essential factors at every stage of the analysis of the causes of these persistent difference. The Fourm's participants' general consensus was that they should be tackled first of all.

Financial implications cannot be separated from the issue of women's employment, whether it is to justify its need or on the contrary to discourage it, or to explain the absence or lack of training of women who are available in the job market. Some examples are:

- In the countries in transition in Central and Eastern Europe companies under pressure to increase profits do not want to maintain social support services, which earlier had backed women's participation in the active population. These pressuress are compelling women to leave the job market as the cost of child care increases.
- In developing countries, especially in Asia, Africa and Latin America, the worsening of poverty and the increase in the number of sigle-parent families are requiring women to turn towards income-generating activities, but the lack of training and dufficult access to credit constitute a major handicap.
- In Thailand, one of the major causes of young village girls resorting to prostitution is the state of poverty of their families, who are unable to afford secondary schooling for them.

Prejudices and Stereotypes

Several examples can also be found in the persisting traditions and stereotypes which are an obstacle in the path of women's march to equality of opportunity in the world of work.

- The Nordic countries, in particular Sweden, have insituted a parental leave which enables either one of the parents to take care of the young children at home; but it can be noted that very few fathers avail themselves of this opportunity.
- The status of a profession falls as the number of women entering it increases; salary levels thus become relatively less competitive. This trend is particularly clear in the teaching professions and in some medical professions.

- Measures of positive action are becoming more and more general. They cannot be successful unless they tackle discrimination on all fronts, together with the fixed ideas that are prevalent on the subject of the sexes. In fact, solutions to the financial problems that women's work causes are themselves going through an evolution in mentalities.

In a highly competitive job market, opportunities available to women are conditioned by the comparative cost of women's labour, as it is perceived by the employer. By virtue of the legislation in force in the majority of countries, the obligations linked to maternity protection and family responsibilities tend to increase the direct costs of women workers; generally, employers bridge this gap by lowering the wages of women or limiting recruitment to childless women. This form of discrimination can also go as far as requiring medical certificates to guarantee sterility.

A Global Programme

To avoid such tendencies, efforts should be channelled toward two fronts. First, evaluating the relationship between a real cost-benefit (including the criterion of effective productivity) with a view toward eliminating the false idea that women workers are more expensive.

Secondly, making sure that in legislation, in practice and especially in the mentality of men and women all around the reproductive function and care of persons are recognized as social functions whose costs should be footed by society as a whole.

Recognizing the universal nature of the problem and the various fronts where one would need to enter into combat, this programme should aim at changing the relationship of power between men and women. For this change to become permanent, it will be necessary to consolidate the ground gained as the process continues.

Remedies should be composed of measures touching upon, among other areas, legislation and its control, access

to jobs, to training and to resources, the reconciling of professional activities with family responsibility, outreach measures to groups of underprivileged women, improvement of information and research, the participation of women in decision-making and the mobilization of public opinion.

Equal Opportunities for Women in the Community

Over half the people in the Indian community are women. The change in women's contribution to society is one of the most striking phenomena of the late twentieth century. But although they have had the law behind them, women have yet to enjoy the equality they are entitled to in theory. Men need to contribute more to family life, while women have yet to make a real impact on decisions affecting the lives of everybody.

Technological advances have meant the decline of employment in manufacturing, and the growing dominance of service industries. This has meant more jobs for women, but not necessarily better working conditions. Most women are still in lower-paid jobs, and most still work mainly with other women in similar jobs and fields. Women are still under-represented in many sectors of industry, the professions and public service.

More and more women are involved in paid work. There is no job they cannot do, and they are entitled to equal pay for equal work, as well as the same terms and conditions at work, and the same opportunities for promotion. Giving women the opportunity to realize their potential in all spheres of society is increasingly important, for all only by involving both sexes to the full can we develop human resources on really democratic lines.

Equal Pay, Equal Opportunities

The right to equal to equal pay for equal work without discrimination based on sex has to be set out. Equal treatment in access to employment, training, promotion and working conditions has to be encouraged. Equal treatment in social security, as well as for the self-employed are very much needed. Rights to maternity leave and pay, and a guarantee of adequate health and safety at work for pregnant women and nursing mothers are very urgent. The government has to encourage good practice on: Positive action, vocational training, childcare, combating unemployment, equal opportunities in schools, integrating women into working life, combating unwanted sexual behaviour at work, education, and updating protective legislation affecting women. There is still a great deal to be done before we can claim women in the community really get a fair deal and a chance to show what they can do.

Women are still often segregated into jobs that are less well-paid than those typically taken by men. They are often well qualified than men, and the jobs they do are often less secure. These are the kinds of inequalities the society must continue to combat and it will do so, as one of the ways of making sure women do not bear the brunt. Quality and quantity in women's employment are very important.

Better Opportunities to Earn a Living

Getting more women into paid work by promoting job opportunities, entrepreneurship and local employment should be the aim. The aim should be to help them fulfil their potential through better education, training and postive action. Upgrading their skills and equipping them with hi-tech know-how is a priority. Another major concern is helping parents juggle work and caring responsibilities via better services and terms of employment.

Getting Women in Positions of Power

It is hard to believe over half the community's population is female, given how little direct influence women have over what happens in our society. In an electoral constituency where half the voters are women, and where concerns for education, family health and food are paramount, both contestants up for election are male, and they speak to a largely male audience. The women, who work long hours and worry and sacrifice for their families and homes, fuss with the tea, hush the children, over on the periphery. If they are there at all. Politics is 'men's business'.

Training to Keep up with the Times

Women need traing if they are to benefit from growth and technological development. A network of training schemes has to be set up to develop training for women, to publicize their needs, promote information exchanges and encourage the involvement of employers and trade unions.

Changing Minds in School

There is no job women cannot do. A working party is looking at ways of encouraging boys and girls to range more widely in the subjects they take in school. It should aim to support teachers trying to avoid reproducing anachronistic stereotypes.

Pregnant women, mothers of new-born babies and nursing mothers should have the peace of mind of knowing they have secure health and social rights. For women who already have to combine their professional life with running a home and looking after children, political activity requires considerable sacrifices. Women would be more ready to take them on if they thought they stood a chance of recognition on a par with men. That is far from being the case. If equal opportunities for women are provided definitely the country will develop at a faster rate.

12

Lightening the Load for Women

Not only do women in India suffer greater poverty than men, they often have little choice but to pass it on the next generation. Investing in women, therefore, is an effective way of building a better economic future for the poor.

Research findings from all sources are confirming what development practitioners have long observed: women are generally worse off economically than men, and the consequences of their poverty are more serious for future generations.

Women's poverty differs from that of men both in degree and in kind: women experience greater poverty and transmit their disadvantage more readily to their children, thus perpetuating the poverty cycle. At the same time, however, they are better able than men to protect children from the consequences of poverty.

It is this close connection between women's and children's fortunes that makes women's poverty a prime target for enlightened development practice. Anti-property policies need to reach poor women both to maximize social return on development investments and minimize the poverty of this and the next generation.

Breaking the Poverty Cycle

Poor women's rising participation in the world of paid work, however, does not necessarily guarantee a destiny of poverty. On the contrary, their earnings can protect children from poverty. Until fairly recently, the prevailing assumption was that any positive income effect of women's employment on children's health and well-being would be offset by negative effects of reduced child care time by working mothers or by the substitution of older siblings in child care. Recent studies, however, indicate a positive effect of women's employment on child health and nutrition. Women prefer to invest meagre earnings on child well-being and underscore the point that the income poor women earn can yield higher social benefits than income earned by men.

These positive effects of poor women's income-earning activities are not necessarily contradictory with the negative effects of women's increased work on their daughter's educational opportunities. It is likely that women need a minimum level of income to act on their preference to invest scarce resources on child well-being, below which their additional work perpetuates rather than halts poverty.

Policy and Research Implications

It is therefore desirable to implement policies that reinforce the virtuous cycle between women's and children's well-being that can occur in poor families when women have more income, and avoid those that can instead trigger a vicious cycle of deprivation between mothers and children. Circumstances which increase poor women's unpaid or very low-paid work can foster the perpetuation of disadvantage. These include the effects of declining household incomes during economic downturns, the decrease in service provision by the State which accompanies structural adjustment programmes, and many community and child-centered interventions that rely heavily on women's unpaid time. Anti-poverty packages need to reinforce poor women's roles as economic producers and avoid actions which increase women's unpaid labour for the promotion of family child welfare.

Projects which increase women's productivity in home and market production and expand their employment options can help to turn the vicious cycle of poverty into a virtuous one. This necessitates executing agencies which can work with women, and budget allocations to strengthen the capacity of institutions to implement and monitor gender-responsive employment programmes for the poor.

The reach of project interventions is restricted, however. Their impact is often short-lived and while they can help to contain the cycle of poverty between mothers and children, they cannot in themselves transform women's economic activities. Changes in the polity environment are required for the latter. These include agricultural policies which target poor farmers and give women farmers access to land, credit and technical assistance; financial policies which promote the growth of small enterprises and foster entrepreneurship among women; and labour-intensive "pro-poor" economic growth policies: In addition, governments need to invest in upgrading women's occupational skills, and in a series of complementary measures, including overhauling social security systems, establishing gender-friendly regulatory frameworks for agricultural and industrial growth, and legislate on child care options.

To guide these policies, we need: research that distinguishes families from households and seeks to understand the formation, structure and dynamics of families headed by women; longitudinal studies which provide a narrative for events in women's lives and assess the transmission of disadvantage between mothers and children; trend data which tracks changes in women's work as a result of changes in economic conditions and in implementation of economic and social policies; and analyses of the mechanics, cost and consequences of targeting interventions to female heads of households and poor women.

The policy-oriented research agenda is perhaps as ambitious as the policy agenda and both require funding. Investing in women should be an effective use of scarce development resources if these actions are guided by the basic principle of seeing women in India for what they are: economic and social agents and not merely passive recipients of welfare.

13

Women and Poverty

It is becoming more evident that the majority of the poor in developed and developing worlds are women. Poverty among rural women is growing faster than among rural men. Over the past 20 years, for example, the number of women in absolute poverty rose by 50 per cent as against some 30 per cent for rural men. The alarming evidence concerning the underlying trends for this process strongly indicates that the gender composition of the poor is veering towards a greater share of women.

Poverty manifests itself in many ways among migrant and refugee women, elderly women and children and indigenous women. Poverty is a complex, diverse and dynamic condition stemming out of depravation with respect to income, from social inferiority, isolation, physical weakness, powerlessness and humiliation.

Analysis of women's poverty suggests that its main causes stem from the perpetual disadvantage of women in terms of their position in the labour market, access to productive resources and income for the satisfaction of their their basic needs. They also demonstrate that poor women possess exceptional resourcefulness, initiative and entrepreneurial spirit and that they show tenacity and self-sacrifice in trying to take a long-term view. of their poor economic conditions and in safeguarding their livelihoods.

Development is the most important challenge facing the human race. The lack of progress in the last twenty years in the eradication of poverty and growing proportion of women among the poor is the single most important threat to the progress of development and its sustainability. As long as three-quarters of the world population continue to suffer from acute depravation, as long as profound imbalances in global consumption continue to persist, and, more important, as long as the spread of poverty, particularly among women, continues unchecked, there can be no development. The history of the development process shows again that the economic status of women is the key variable in the solution to the poverty crisis. It is time for the full recognition of the fact that women are part of the solution to poverty and to the stagnating development, not part of the problem.

The Earth Summit in Rio, the Human Rights Conference in Vienna, the Population Conference in Cairo and the Beijing conference all were milestone events in terms of advancing our understanding of the crucial role of women in development and focusing the attention of the international community on the issues concerning the role of women in the work place and in society. All of them drew attention to women's full and effective participation in development. None, however, fully artirculated how to achieve this challenging task.

It is important to retain focus on the issue of economic potential when discussing poverty among women because it is clear that power is only meaning something in practical terms if it is reinforced by economic power. Women have the means to transform productive resources into such power if only enabling environment is created. It is not the lack of capabilities, but that of resources which is clearly responsible for women's poverty.

Sometimes the so badly needed resources are not even truly scarce. Billions have been wasted on arms purchases around the globe and particularly in the countries which cannot afford such misallocation of public funds. At the same time, women's organizations from grassroots to the international level are poorly funded. Such misallocation of resources at the time when poverty among women is increasing, is immoral and unacceptable, not only on the part of the governments which pursue such wasteful policies, but also on the part of the suppliers, who in most cases are developed economies.

Government's responsibilities do not end here. It is extremely important, and indeed it is the main duty of every government around the world, to provide a conducive environment for economic growth and stability by pursuing responsible and sound macro-economic policies which will enable the economy to grow without marginalizing women. When inflation is rampant, when political climate is unstable, leading to conflicts and civil strife, little can be done for poverty alleviation.

14

Women in Authority

The Ideal and the Reality

At the current rate of progress it will take a very long time to bring about equality in sharing decision-making between men and women in all areas. In terms of human rights and social justice, such equality is absolutely vital; it is also the best way to promote change with a human face. Would the world be a better place if women had equal access to management positions.

A Near Absence

Almost everywhere in the world, women have the vote and account for over half of the electorate. With but rare exceptions, however, their political activities are restricted to anonymous and informal roles in local communities. They hover at the margins of the higher levels of trade union, political, governmental and corporate life, and of interest groups. Until 1987, women occupied barely 10 per cent of parliamentary seats. The same holds true for the trade unions, despite the fact that women account for nearly one-third of union memberships. Indeed, the women to have reached the leadership of a trade union can be counted on the fingers of one hand. This pattern of inequality is mirrored, indeed accentuated, in the employers' organizations, where women are practically absent. Everyone knows the situation in professional employment. Women continue to be concentrated in lower-qualified, lower-paid jobs, and very few manage to attain managerial posts, though the trend is on the increase.

Lower-paid Jobs

The "invisibility" of women in public life, and consequently in political, economic and professional activity, is both the cause and consequence of their being consistently barred from positions of authority. The way in which cultural and social models repeat themselves creates a setting that is hardly conducive to women progressing much beyond the limits of their homes and immediate working and living environment. Enmeshed in a tangle of little encouragement and probable reprobation, women are hesitant about struggling to advance in professional or political careers, as to do so would frequently put at stake the subordinate role that hitherto atleast guaranteed them a secure position within the family circle. On the other hand, as they hardly manage to participate fully in the decisions affecting their lives and families, it will prove difficult for them to break out of the vicious circle.

Rights and Obstacles

Why is it then essential for women to play an equal role in decision-making? One can approach this objective from three points of view. First , it is a clear question of human rights: women make up half the population and more than one-third of the workforce and so their right to full citizenship and equality of opportunity and treatment in employment must be clearly expressed by their participation in all levels of activity. Secondly, it is a matter of social justice to combat discrimination against women, which is at its very harshest when it comes to employment. Thirdly, it is an essential requirement for the acceleration and effectiveness of development, as women are capable of providing a different sort of ability and creativity, which has not so far been tapped, and they can ensure a better balance in the allocation of resources and distribution of the benefits of progress.

Two Types of Obstacles

There are two types of obstacles to be overcome in order that women can have access to decision-making positions—structural and situational. They include the famous differences in levels of education, occupational experience and income levels as compared to men. These combine with and are reinforced by the situational factors such as the burden of family responsibilities, legal, psychological and material dependence on their spouses and male relatives, colleagues or bosses, and the fact that society is not prepared to change its attitudes and support women in assuming positions of responsibility. The deeply rooted "gender ideology" underlying all this constitutes a system of barriers to the upper echelons. It takes the form of values, attitudes and behavioural patterns which inhibit development and the recognition of the leadership qualities of women and which thus demand additional sacrifices from those who nevertheless strive to overcome them.

Additional Sacrifices

It has been estimated that women's participation in excess of 30 per cent in the upper echelons would be necessary for any noticeable difference to be made to the nature and tenor of the decisions taken in the areas affected. So what would this difference be? Women tend to speak with a "different voice" which as a rule lays stress on the social ethos of development, that is to say education, health, children, environment, dialogue and peace. Conversely, men tend to concentrate on the economic aspects such as production, trade, profitability, finance, technology and national defence. If we really aspire to any development of the human lot involving both economic growth and social equity, the best way to achieve this coveted objective will be by having men and women sharing in decision-taking.

15

Promotion of Women

Women made up more than half the world's population, produced 80 per cent of its food, laboured for two-thirds of its working hours, were paid 10 per cent of its income and owned one per cent of its property.

These figures conceal manifold forms of the disadvantaging and discrimination of women. Such as the unjust division of burdens in families, the economic exploitation of women, the loss of their control over resources, and finally the unequal rating of paid and unpaid work. The latter, in the form of work for the family, on the land, for the community towards improving local living conditions, and nursing the old and the sick, adds up-mostly to a 14 to 16 hour working day. True, employment of women has increased further everywhere in the world. But a number of them work in unsafe and socially unsecured conditions. They are also poorly paid and as a rule have hardly any chances to better themselves. Many women can earn money only in urban informal sectors or farming.

Global Public for Women

To be sure, the Decade of the Women (1976 to 1985), the adoption of the convention on eliminating every form of discrimination against women (1979), the key role of women in the development process and their rights have created a global public for them. Moreover, their activities have got underway a reorientation of international policies on women. But, despite numerous progressive international moves in the area of formal legislation, the political debates on the legal status of women are in no way over.

Making general statements on the correlation of the impacts of social development and the situation of women is difficult because the political, economic and cultural framework conditions differ greatly from one country to another. However, discrimination against women manifests itself in most traditional as well as modern societies as a structural feature. Nowhere in the world are women treated "as good" as men, and all countries slip on the scale of human development when inequality between the sexes is measured. Differences between the life situations and opportunities of men and women sill arise from unequal possibilities of access to employment, income, economic resources, health care, food, education and training.

Social developments such as fundamental changes in traditional family and social structures, migration, urbanization, the contrast between traditional and "modern" ways of life, and often unfavourable economic developments for the majority of the people have a great influence on the role of the women in the various third world countries. Moreover, the increasing differentiation of the South in terms of poorer and richer countries cannot obscure the fact that in the 1990s the general social conditions for the majority of women have not improved.

Almost one-third of all the people in the countries of the South live in life-threatening poverty, and the overwhelming majority of those are women. Female poverty has different aspects such as poverty of income, low literacy, a lack of vocational training and the poverty of old age.

Furthermore, the continuing legal pluralism in many societies impeded efforts to achieve equality of status for women. Although in many countries men and women are meanwhile equal according to the constitution and legislation, there is still a great contradiction between constitutionally guaranteed rights and reality. According to religious law or custom, women in many countries are not equal to men. That means they have no property rights, or may not sign any contracts without their husbands' and constitutional rights, this implies the danger of becoming poor, particularly for single mothers, divorcees or widows.

Against this background it is no surprise that women are under-represented at political decision-taking levels, in government posts, political parties, trade unions and associations. The structures of many institutions give little support to women's interests, and managerial positions are held almost exclusively by men. In part, women-specific measures are seen as a compulsory exercise and, at best, tolerated as a fad.

New Opportunities

But in general the radical changes taking place in many countries open new opportunities for police on women. On the one land, this is because the extent of the disadvantaging and suppression of women is more visible. And, on the other, because the fields of work for women have become wider—if mainly in urban centres. In some countries, women have been able to push through binding legal regulations (election laws, political party statutes, women's quota rules for local councils), in order to guarantee their stronger participation in parties and trade unions. With the programme slogans of "empowerment" and "redistribution of power", women who are organized in self-help organizations, associations, networks and political parties are demanding participation in political decision processes and access to the political institutions. They are striving for social power in a bid to influence the factors which cause discrimination against them.

The transition from authoritarian to democratic forms of government in a great number of countries has placed women's organizations in a changed environment. There are now countless such bodies, and their combined clout is changing the status of women and helping to broaden their scope for social action. But in some countries women are still faced with considerable difficulties in organizing themselves with formal status.

On account of progressive impoverishment, however, it women's newly-won scope for action and shaping their lives is markedly cramped. Current developments such as religious fundamentalism or economic recession have inhibiting impacts on new approaches to policies on women. In part, one must speak of a "backlash". Even where the legal position of women has been improved they have not been able to assert their social, economic and political rights. In some countries, it's feared that only elitist women's organizations will have a chance to break into the political process.

16

Empowerment for Women?

Actually, the situation of women has changed completely in the last 30 years. At the beginning of the 1970s women were a blind spot in both development aid and the debate on it. The promotion of women is now established in all state institutions and non-governmental organisations (NGOs). Gender training is to sensitive development workers to take a gender-specific approach in analysing development processes, carrying out statistical surveys, and planning and evaluating activities.

From Integration to Empowerment

Those women who in the 1970s criticised development polity and its actors for being one-eyed must now see themselves as line-prompters and idea-providers. All the terms they used have been adopted in official usage. The image of the woman has changed from being a Cinderella-like, hard-done-by person, the poor soul, the victim, to a dynamic, reliable actor with apparently inexhaustible reserves of energy and creativity to bring to bear in a development process that has got stuck. The concept of empowerment has replaced the old "integration in development" approach in the promotion of women. And the women's approach (gender and development). This calls for the inclusion of men, taking a close look at the gender relationship and changing it into the long run.

All this undoubtedly progress which illuminates the blind spot. So is that enough to please women critics of the male-dominated development-aid scene and female lobbyists for the promotion of women? Have they achieved what they wanted? That is, a policy on women which on the one hand takes up their practical, everyday needs, but on the other works strategically towards eliminating the hierarchy between the genders by structural changes? The fact is that one must differentiate between what governments, multilateral institutions and NGOs are saying and what they are doing.

Redistribution of Social Power and Control of Resources

The empowerment concept makes clear the political and economic gap between man and women, it aims at a redistribution of social power and control of resources in favour of women based on a development strategy which is no longer oriented on growth, the world market and military power.

The concept has had seemingly record acceptance in the executive suites and programmes of the governments while at the same time its substance has been drastically diluted. Taken on board hook-line-and-sinker by official polity, its politically critical teeth—namely posing the power question—have been extracted. It now has no bite critical of development and social policy. It just stands modestly and harmlessly for every strengthening and participation of women.

Professionalization on the NGOs side and state orientation on the grassroots have brought activities nearer to one another. The modes of expression are identical. But where are women really at the centre of development practice? And where are they at the centre of developmental organizations? The promotion of women is still an appendage to development policy, including in most NGOs. That is shown not only by the low number of "pure" women's projects, but also by the subordinate role of women's interests and measures for women in integrated programmes. Defined as a "cross-sectoral task", the advancement of women is often reduced to the mere addition of a woman competent. For example, in the form of small-scale loans for sewing machines. The few women in the organizations are assigned a low-ranking and sparsely-equipped niche.

Lack of Long-term Strategy

The gender approach has made the yawning gap between rhetoric and practice even bigger. It might be useful as an instrument of analysis, if it is not debased to a technocratic checklist. But no one at present knows for sure how it can be implemented. The international trend is to implement promotion of women less in "pure" women's projects than to integrate it in other activities. Parallel to that, there are signs of a trend in which the women's or gender sections of development agencies are being disbanded and integrated in country or specialist sections. Currently, however, there is apparently still a lack of concepts for implementing a strategically oriented advancement of women. If integration, or "mainstreaming" now takes place at the various levels, it is to be feared that the promotion of women will peter out rather than spread.

At the same time, disenchantment prevails among those who have understood that the advancement of women is a means to more rights and opportunities in life, more self-confidence and social recognition. The demand to effect structural change through projects founders on the general conditions. Like development assistance as a whole, raising the status of women is also in many regions becoming increasingly merely disaster relief and survival aid. All involved have long known there are no universally applicable formulas for projects, and still fewer handy "directions for use" for getting out of poverty and blasting open patriarchal suppression.

The dilemma is clear. The economic crisis, the over-indebted and socially inactive governments, and the men who steal away from responsibility are saddling women with ever increasing burdens in securing survival. Thereby the women urgently need support. At the same time, the limited impacts of promotional measures, or even their boomerang effect, are becoming more obvious.

Many women are being catapulted into the exploitation mechanisms of the market and money economy only when they get involved in projects. Or, at least, the projects are speeding that process. Because of the projects the women neglect subsistence production and their traditional principles of the moral economy. But it is also clear that as a result of training programmes, new forms of organization, development of new fields of action, and mobility, women's groups would collapse.

Thus, the old dilemma—of here a policy of small steps necessary for survival, and their big strategic and structural concepts—has got worse. But there's no way around it: the advancement of women must continue to seek bridges between being content with little and the vision of a development that is more just to women.

Population Growth and Women's Role in India

We have limited economic resources. There is a pressing need to abolish poverty. If population grows unchecked, abolition of poverty becomes very difficult. Due to the rise in population, illiteracy is growing as educational facilities are not expanding as fast as the population. Though employment facilities are being provided, we are not able to solve the unemployment problem. Though production and national income are rising, standard of living is not rising at the same rate. This growing population remains a serious drawback.

Conventional wisdom holds that slowing population growth is the key to solving a vast array of social, economic, and environmental problems. To be sure, in a world of finite resources, unlimited growth in the number of people requiring food, shelter, and work, not to mention access to natural resources, cannot be sustained. But the increasingly singular focus on demographics simply deflects attention from the fundamental social conditions—poverty, inequity, and the abject status of women—of which population growth is not the cause, but the consequence.

In India, as in much of the world, women are last in line for education, job training, credit, and sometimes even food—despite the fact that raising the status of women is the most effective way both to reduce birth and to achieve higher standards of health and economic productivity.

In India's tradition-bound society, where childbearing is often the only route to status and security, the majority of women have little to gain from having fewer children. The government, by contrast, is bent on cutting birthrates in half over the next decade, but has shown little commitment to meeting women's needs. And so a vicious cycle is perpetuated. As long as the status of women remains low, voluntary family planning efforts will continue to flounder, tempting the government to use pressure to meet its demographic goals.

India will surpass China as the world's most populous country by the middle of the next century. Each day the number of people who lack access to adequate food, health care, housing, clean water, and education spirals upward.

Female Education

Female education is the single most influential determinant of both lower birth rates and increasing empowerment for women.

Indian society manages to devote fewer resources to educating its girls than its boys. At the household level, cultural restrictions on female behaviour combined with the need for cheap household labour create a sharp gender gap in literacy. In both the Hindu and Moslem traditions, for example, notions of female "modesty" and "purity" dictate that unmarried females remain separate from unrelated males. Because the bulk of India's teachers are men, and most schools educate boys and girls under the same roof, many traditional families keep their daughters home, regardless of their income. Moreover, parents are apt to invest in educating girls only when they perceive that long-term gains will outweigh immediate costs.

For the impoverished majority, the expense of sending a girl to school—paying for uniforms, books, is prohibitive especially when young girls are required to work at home and in the fields.

Women's lack of knowledge translates directly into poor nutrition and health for themselves and their offspring. In turn, these conditions cause high infant mortality—for which many women compensate by having more babies.

Nutrition and Health

Nutritional and health status is also marked by gender disparity. Both boys and girls in India are nutritionally disadvantaged, as nearly half of the country's households fail to provide even the minimum daily caloric requirements. But malnutrition is far more prevalent among females than males. From birth, male children consistently receive more and better food than their sisters, event though the nutritional needs of prepubescent boys and girls are virtually identical. Boys, given the same level of illness, are taken to doctors more often than girls. As a result of this neglect, far more girls than boys die in the critical period between infancy and age five.

Discrimination in feeding and health care produces one of India's most provocative signs of gender bias: In fact, the ratio of women to men in the country has been declining.

Women and Family Income

Son preference and the subsequently biased allocation of family resources is based on a series of myths the Indian government has failed to combat. One is the notion—not peculiar to India—that females do not contribute to family income. Throughout the world, women bear the "invisible" burdens of unpaid domestic work and childbearing, the economic value of which is rarely reflected by official statistics.

Young girls in India generally work longer hours than boys of the same age. By age 10, girls in low income families are working eight or more hours a day assisting their mothers by tending siblings, collecting water and firewood, herding small animals, weeding fields, or facing the daily grind of low-paid child labour in the marketplace.

The poorer the family, the more vital the economic contribution that women and girls make, especially in the growing number of female-headed households.

Indifference Towards Women

The attempts to enhance agricultural productivity disproportionate benefit men.

Expansion of the irrigated area allocated to cash corps, such as groundnut and cotton, has come at the expense of food crops on which women depend to feed their families. And while the mechanization of plowing and levelling that comes with these projects reduces the traditional workload of men, that for women actually increases. Women still must carry out by hand the tasks of weeding, turning soil, and harvesting, but over much larger areas.

The result is to deepen women's poverty and enhance the perceived value of having many children to help with chores.

Not surprisingly, the share of married couples of reproductive age using contraceptives—now 40 per cent—is low, and most of these are older couples who turned to sterilization (counted as a form of contraceptive) only after having large families.

This bleak situation is shadowed by an ominous fact of history. Past attempt to reduce births in the absence of social changes enhancing women's status have been accompanied by increases in violence against females—in the beating and abandonment of women who don't bear sons, in female infanticide and child neglect, and in the rising use of abortion for sex-selection.

Experience shows that even in India, with its immense tangle of troubles, well-designed programmes can produce dramatic improvements in family health while improving women's status and reducing births.

Increasing young girls' access to education and offering older women a chance for learning are essential to increasing female autonomy. Requisite steps include serious efforts to train and hire more female teachers, to set up literacy and tutoring campaigns in every state, and to encourage the growth of women's empowerment groups to foster changes at the village level. These strategies already have been proven in the southern state of Kerala, internationally lauded for its dramatic gains in the health and economic status of women and in slowing population growth.

Equally important are broad public education campaigns to raise awareness of the immense value of women's work and welfare to families and societies. The mass media also could be enlisted in the effort to change dramatically social perceptions of women's roles by depicting positive images of women and their economic contribution to society.

Much of the battle to win recognition of the importance of women's lives and health to socieites will have to be fought by women themselves. Indications are that women are responding to the challenge.

By filling the existing demand for quality voluntary family planning services, the government can make cuts in birthrates of at least 25 per cent over the next decade, thereby starting the process toward reducing the country's population. Equally critical to a long termstrategy of sustainable development is a sustained political commitment to improve the status of women throughout India. Only by working toward all of these objectives simultaneously can the dreams of women for full partnership in society come true.

18

No Progress without a Secular Society

Every day, women continue to be victims of rape, trafficking, acid-throwing, dowry deaths and other kinds of torture. At the opening of this new century, women are still not considered as equal human beings in many parts of the world. Religion and patriarchy continue to have an all-encroaching hold on their lives, maintaining and justifying their age-old oppression. In some South Asian societies, this hold is even increasing.

I do not believe that there can be real equality in a society dominated by religion. Western countries speak repeatedly about the necessity of economic development to alleviate poverty. But this is not enough. Some oil-rich countries may be economically developed, but women are deprived of all rights. The supremacy of religion is incompatible with freedom of expression, women's rights and democracy. This is why I see religion as the main enemy of women's development.

We have to act on several fronts at once. First of all, improving access to education. In a society like Bangladesh, 80 per cent of women are illiterate. For centuries women have been taught they are the slaves of men. It is very hard to change their minds, to make them aware of their oppression, to give them a sense of their independence. This educational effort has to go hand in hand with a secular feminist movement in society. Such movements have to start within the country and they cannot take hold when people are uneducated and unaware of their oppression. I'm not sure you can accomplish much from the outside, except to expose in the media the atrocities women in all too many countries face in their day-to-day lives.

In some countries, this movement is emerging, but very timidly, and it has a slim margin of manoeuvre. It has the uphill task of fighting for the repeal of religious laws and the introduction of a uniform civil code. So far, it tends to be constituted by a few individual feminists who are forced to be diplomatic, to compromise with fundamentalists, be they men or women. But they are trying to change the system, step by step, and it will take a very long time. People are not yet ready to do away with religious laws that impact upon every aspect of society, from education and health to the workplace and the home.

For women's status to change, we also need enlightened leaders who believe in equality. In countries of South Asia women with a strong voice do not have the support of political leaders, whether they be men or women. Look at the counties in which women are in politics, or even heads of state. Does it follow that women in those countries are emancipated? Because of long-standing vested interests, such leaders continue to back measures that oppress women. They are not ideologically committed to changing these conditions. In South Asia, most of the women who become heads of state are religious, and like men, they adhere to the religious objectives of the Establishment. Until a society is not based on religion and women and considered equal to men before the law, I do not think that politics will advance the cause of women.

Until a society is not based on religion and women are considered equal to men before the law, I do not think that politics will advance the cause of women. In Western countries, women are educated, they are treated equally, they have access to jobs. In these conditions, their participation in politics has a meaning.

Education, a secular feminist movement, and leaders—both men and women—committed to equality and justice. This is what it will take to change the dire conditions which too many women still face today. It will take a very long time, but we are here to work towards that end.

19

On the Way to Commercial Microcredits

The Changing of Development Instrument

The founding of financial institutions in the developing countries, whose target groups are supposed to be poorer people and, in particular, income-generating micro, small-scale and medium-sized enterprises, originated in the industrialised nations. Soon after Western "development policy" began in the 1950s and 1960s the donor noted that investment in infrastructure was insufficient to achieve growth. Reflecting on the experiences of Europe, state or mixed-enterprise development banks were founded in many developing countries with the support of various donors. The banks were to promote industrialisation as a substitution for imports, as well as farming, housing construction and regional development. Their common feature was that they combined the characteristics of a bank and a public authority. On the one hand, they managed loan holdings and handled payment transactions, and one the other they "prompted" development by non-repayable grants. Since these functions each followed a very different logic, the banks were required to undertake a difficult tightrope walk.

Exclusion of Small Borrowers

As a justification for the existence of state banks, even in liberal market economies people like to point out, and rightly so, that normal commercial banks would have scarcely any interest in the business of the "small fry" and, that they also shun longer-term financing of investment. A lender cannot beforehand tell the difference between good and less good borrowers, and must set a uniform interest rate for his credit offer. In order not to lose his cost-efficient and low risk customers, meaning to avoid what the economists call "adverse selection", he sets the interest rate not as high as he would have to in covering his costs in the case of small borrowers, and "rations" his loans according to criteria such as reputation, collateral and business volume. Even in an otherwise completely liberalised model world, small borrowers remain excluded from formal bank loans even if they would be able and prepared to bear cost-covering terms. That applies to an even because, other being equal, in most countries of the world they have lower incomes than men and also are discriminated against in access to property rights.

Therefore, in microeconomic terms, the idea behind the founding of development banks is well-founded. However, the design of the institutional structures, including the governance structure, requires a fine balancing of the bank and public authority functions in order to reconcile efficiency, cost-covering and the promotion mission. All too often, the easy way out for all involved is to combine the negative features of bank and public authority, meaning linking profit-mongering and the exclusion of small borrowers with a subsidy mentality and politisation. As critical studies from the 1970s showed, following the initial euphoria, development banks seldom live up to their promises.

For the donor institutions, however, these banks are ideal counterparts absorbing financial and technical assistance. Thanks to their banking function in payment transactions, they practically never have outflow problems. In addition, they can at any time produce from their broad portfolios the projects demanded by a donor or; his client, such as parliamentary committee. And promoting development banks also promotes the exports of the donors, meaning the industrialised nations.

An important point of criticism focuses on this "hidden" promotion of exports. This is that micro, small-scale and medium-size enterprises mostly do not need a great deal of imports, and especially not so long as they are still building a trusting relationship with their bank to overcome the asymmetrical information mentioned above. So they need loans in local rather than foreign currency.

When favourably-priced foreign currency loans are available for projects which a bank public authority or company would in any case implement or promote, these can be used for other purposes, such as for imports of consumer goods or other agreeable things which otherwise could not be afforded. So who can blame politicians, bureaucrats, bank directors or companies when they prove to be fervent supporters of the financing of development banks!

Critics of the development bank system did not have an easy task in asserting themselves against the concerted interest of individuals on both the donor and recipient sides. But the search for alternatives began on a broad front in the 1980s.

Alternatives to Development Bank Promotion

Committed politicians, bureaucrats, academics, consultants and NGOs in various countries around the world began to get down to serious work in forming a new policy. Their efforts were based on the declared principles of poverty alleviation and sustainability in institution-building in promoting micro, small-scale and medium-scale enterprises via the finance sector. The results were published in the World Bank's World Development Report of 1989.

In an initial step, so-called "integrated" rural and urban projects and programmes were equipped with their own "rotation funds" which were to finance employment and income-generating measures. However, due to their integration in projects focussed on infrastructure measures such as slum clearance, irrigation, electrification, public health services and regional planning, they degenerated typically into drawing funds for projects management's. That meant that a recipient mentality rather than a sustainable financial service provider structure came into being, and the mixing of loans and free gifts undermined rather than promoted a positive attitude towards market conform financial relationships.

The Grameen Bank in Bangladesh is a special case. Here, the charismatic professor Muhammed Yunus persuaded the government to place a state bank in the service of poverty alleviation, and for landless women in particular. The results are not undisputed, especially since the bank is still very dependent upon subsidies. But this institution shows that participation in the monetary economy is anything but a matter of course, and that emancipation of women as free economic citizens is a goal to which purely technological financial principles should perhaps be subordinated. The Grameen Bank has yet to stand the test of developing into a sustainable institution without a heroic head and without subsides. Maybe it will really show now a poor country like Bangladesh can establish itself in the long term as a "funnel" for permanent development assistance transfers. But a final assessment does not appear to be possible at present.

The NGOs are another alternative to customary development banks. Donors like to promote them because they are close to the target groups, or at least are able to portray themselves so. In practice, however, they prove to be problematical partners when it comes to developing a durable formal finance structure in the interests of small borrowers. As committed left-wingers, NGO members and leaders usually take a sceptical stance towards the market and its "bourgeois" laws. They are seldom willing to act as bankers with all necessary toughness and assume the "ownership" of a financial institution.

Critical evaluations show that in some cases NGOs can be persuaded to found financial institutions and also run them as sole or co-owners. But the success of such upgrading projects depends very much upon the consultants and donors, and above all upon the existence of a capable leader. They cannot, however, be regarded as a norm.

The target groups and the academics advising them on-site noticed after a while, of course, that the big words were hollow. They realised that first and foremost it was matter of the hidden agenda of the national and international financiers and not particularly about reducing poverty among the target groups. If the "frontier" of the formal finance sector was to be pushed downwards in the direction of the poor, what they really needed in financial services had to be made available to them. These were small, readily available operating funds and emergency loans and secure and worthwhile investment options for temporary financial surpluses. Since poverty was a mass phenomenon, these financial products had to be offered with a loan technology, meaning a form of organisation, that gave them a mass reach with as much saturation as possible.

The then prevailing pattern was "controlled investment loan", involving obligatory consultancy, subsidised interest rates and relatively large sums to push through innovations in the context of "pilot projects" which, however, due to limited subsidy funds, never got beyond the promotion of a few "pilots". So the reforms diagnosis meant a radical change. But there were enough people on either side of the political "barricades" who became convinced by this plausible if hardy grandiose concept. As a self-supporting commercial system which nevertheless was in the interests of the target groups, it began to assert itself towards the end of the 1990s under the label of "commercial approach" or "new development finance".

After the Fall of the Berlin Wall

With the fading of utopic vision, empirically-based diagnoses gained ground and showed that precisely an unpretentious and reliable bank-customer relationship was the best contribution a bank could make to economic survival. In addition, they also demonstrated that in many cases a bank could in fact also help the target group of poor people, and particularly micro- and small-scale enterprises, to accumulate assets. Furthermore, it should not only be mentioned but even emphasised that there were, and should be, public services of all kinds, including old age pensions, family allowance and similar transfers. Which counter poverty around the world. That was necessary to prevent microcredit programmes and similar bank services facing a demand they could not meet. Taking out a loan and servicing it with interest and repayment of the capital sum is always a burden for the borrower, and possible a benefit only insofar as it enables a special opportunity for profit to be seized. For the poorest of the poor, transfers are called for not loans and other bank or insurance services.

Development cooperation practicians on the ground and ideologically unbiased theorists alike came to these conclusions as early as the mid-1980s. But the ideological pressure did not ease until after the collapse of the East Bloc, when both the communist threat and the utopia of the non-capitalist workers' and farmers' paradise disappeared.

So it is not surprising that shortly afterwards the practicians of both sides and the immediate representatives of the target groups got together with enlightened representatives of donors, consultants and academics to form an international coalition titled "New Development Finance". The Microcredit Summit of 1997 with Hilary Clinton had already leaned in this direction, even if it still sent no clear signal in regard to the issue of dependency on subsidies. But the donors gave a green light for a massive financial promotion. World Bank President James Wolfensohn promised that together with all the other summit participants he would go all to ensure that by 2005 and additional 100 million families around the world would have microcredits.

The subsequent "Annual Conferences on New Development Finance", which took place at the University of Frankfurt Main from 1997 to 1999, than developed into an important forum at which formerly diametrically opposed actors joined forces against the "ancient regime", According to their definition, "old" is everything which boils down to the demand of re-educating people and coupling loans with obligatory consultancy. In the long term, that results in dependency on subsidies, becoming hostage to the political games of influential national rulers and donors, and loses sight of the declared target group of the urban and rural poor. All this applies mainly to smaller countries which receive heavy international assistance. In India, Pakistan and Brazil, not to mention China, the conditions have their own rhythms and special features.

After the end of communism there was a new situation not only in the developing countries and the North-South relationship, but also and above all in Eastern Europe. Established donor institutions such as USAID and the Reconstruction Loan Corporate (KfW) were supplemented by the multilateral European Bank for Reconstruction and Development (EBRD), and what were soon to be called "transformation Countries" lined up with the "classic" recipients of international development aid.

Internationally operating NGOs and consultancies with experience if the microcredit systems of developing countries were not also called for to assist the projects and programmes in Eastern Europe. The finance sector was perceived as the core of every market economy. At the same time, the donors soon recognised the importance of small to medium-sized business, trades, small holders and all the many disparate micro and small-scale enterprises for employment and the supply of the population. However, financial services were not available to any great degree to cover their needs.

It could now be seen that payment transactions did not function without commercial banks, and that this shortcoming had a considerable negative impact on small enterprises. Going beyond microcredits, which until then had always been the main instrument of financial assistance, the focus was now on deposits, transfers and all the other financial services that were important for the target groups. "Microfinancing" gradually became the generic term for the orientation of financial sector measures to benefit the "small people".

"Downscaling" or "Starting from Scratch"

By means of special loan programmes, which were kept separate from the other portfolios, the external donors sought at first to persuade the existing banks to downscalr their activities and address the newly emerging small to medium-size businesses in the private sector. On balance, the result was rather meager, for these programmes did little to influence the characteristics of the Eastern European commercial banks. And every time some of them were privatised or had to be shut down due to financial rows or corruption scandals, it affected the special small enterprises portfolios regardless of how efficiently they were managed.

Besides using this channel via the big banks, donors also began building up loan programmes through NGOs and local chambers of commerce. The results here were also disappointing, for local implementing organisations are mostly unsuitable for a susbstanstible mass banking business.

But senior officials and executive at donors and consultancies soon had the idea of founding their own micro-finance institutes. "Starting from scratch" green field banking and similar terms began to make the rounds. The first "Micro-enterprise Bank" came into being in Bosnia and soon afterwards other micro-finance institutions (MFIs) were founded.

Unlike customary development cooperation projects, which have a timeframe, the MFIs are open-ended, and consultants in the North also see themselves as long-term partner. In contrast, international development organisations are more and more becoming second-class partners from which local bodies must sooner or later separate themselves again to avoid being left in the lurch. After all, their cooperation has a time limit, and they will leave the country again.

In view of the challenges of globalisation, the banks should perhaps consider using their development projects to establish a network of long-term investments and thus fulfil their promotion mission in favour of the "small people" not only locally and nationally, but also globally.

Measuring Population's Impact

There is no easy way to measure the overall impact of human activities on the environment. Nevertheless, several approaches have been developed as follows:

Environmental Resource Accounting

Environmental resource accounting attempts to place an economic value on "environmental goods and services" used-natural resources that conventionally have been regarded as free and used in common. These include unpolluted freshwater clean air, ocean life, forests, and wetlands.

Some economists argue that the value of environmental goods and services should be incorporated into estimates of gross manufactured capital, which depreciates in value overtime, environmental capital (such as forests, fisheries, and unpolluted air and water) currently is not considered to depreciate, and no charge is made against current income as it is used. A country could exhaust its mineral resources, cut down its forests, erode its soils, pollute its acquires, and hunt its wildlife and fisheries to extinction, but measured income would not be affected as the natural assets disappeared.

If natural resources were valued in the same way that manufactured assets are valued, it might help economies learn to use them more efficiently and to conserve them in order to assure continued use in the future. Such valuations also might help indicate the economic benefits of protecting the environment, as well as the ecological benefits. In other terms, instead of continuing to draw down their "environmental capital" until it is gone, economies could begin to live on its interest, maintaining the capital for use indefinitely in the future.

I = P X A x T

The equation I = P x A x T represents another effort to describe the overall impact of humanity on the environment. In the equation:

- I is environmental impact
- P is population (including size, growth, and distribution)
- A is the level of affluence (consumption per capita), and
- T is the level of technology.

Despite its limitations—for instance, inability to assign actual values to each component or to depict changes in the factors over time— the equation is valuable. In particular, it emphasizes that developing countries with large and rapidly growing populations affect the environment, even though their levels of affluence may be low, while at the same time countries in the developed world with little or no population growth have substantial environmental impact because consumption per capita is so high.

The equation makes clear that slowing population growth is a key part of any strategy to reduce humanity's impact on the environment. For example, even if per capita resource consumption (A) declined or technologies (T) improved enough to reduce the environmental impact (I) of humanity by 10 per cent, this gain would be wiped out in less than a decade because world population (P) is growing at over 1 per cent per year since per capita consumption of resources is expected to increase as living standards rise, protecting the environment requires more efficient production technologies, less waste, and ultimately a stable world population size.

Ecological Footprints of Nations

Every body has an impact on the Earth, because they

consume the products and services of nature. Their ecological impact corresponds to the amount o nature they occupy to keep them going. In other words, we calculate the 'ecological footprints' of these countries.

Carrying Capacity

The term "carrying capacity" refers to the number of people the earth can support. Logically, population growth must stop at some point, or the earth would become overcrowded and its resources eventually would be depleted. But what is this maximum human population?

This question has been debated since 1798, when English economists Thomas Malthus predicted that population growth inevitably would outstrip the food ad water supply at some point. Since the estimates of carrying capacity have varied a great deal depending on what assumptions are made out technology, consumption levels, and other factors that are not easily forecast. Some have even argued that the earth's carrying capacity may already have been exceeded in the sense that the world consumed at the rate that Americans and Western Europeans consume.

While no body can know how many people the earth could support, few would want to find out the hard way—by reaching this theoretical limit. Calculate the maximum number of people who could exist on earth seems less important than determining how resources can be used wisely and managed sustainably to improve living standard without eventually destroying the natural environment that supports life itself.

21

All Human Rights for All

The end of the millennium has seen some remarkable advances in political democracy. Oppressed peoples everywhere are at last, or once again, tasting freedom. They owe these victories largely to themselves, to the intelligence, determination, and even the genius of their citizens.

But this freedom will be fragile as long as it is cast in a single mold, the vehicle of a uniform globalization which speaks with a single voice, primarily that of commerce. Principles may be universal; the mechanisms that infuse life into them are shaped by a host of features that are specific to each society.

No vision of democracy—which transcends politics and includes economic, social and cultural life can—really take root if it is a sterile copy that fails to take account of the history and myths, the values and traditions of each people. While these roots are necessary, however, they provide no justification for citing "cultural relativism" as an excuse for violating the basic principles on which the rights of human beings are founded. Respect for "cultural identity" cannot legitimize anti-democratic practices.

A second danger arises from the fact that the field in which these rights are elaborated and exercised is all to often limited. The recent commemoration of the Universal Declaration of Human Rights was a reminder that human rights comprise not only political and civil rights but also, on exactly the same basis, economic and social rights, such as the right to a job, housing, health and education.

One and a half billion people live in dire poverty. Their most fundamental right, the right to life, the bedrock of all other rights, is constantly threatened. So the still unfinished struggle to extend and strengthen human rights includes the duty to promote development.

This duty is not only a matter of legal formalism or an ethical imperative. Fundamental freedoms will remain very fragile as long as poverty, exclusion and inequalities persist. The forces of globalization encourage the establishment of the rule of law, but a version of law biased in favour of rules needed for successful business activity. They also do more to sharpen economic and social tensions rather than to reduce them.

The momentum created by efforts to establish the rule of law in a growing number of countries is coming up against a major obstacle. The principles and rules that govern international relations are increasing their influence on the lives of nations, but they are very far indeed from being democratic. The strongest still hold sway.

This is true where individual states are concerned. They feel their wings have been clipped, and see their legitimate prerogatives being eroded by the rise of kind of a private-sector absolutism, which tends to limit the functions of government to security and mediation, paralyzing its role as the guarantor of the general interest and depriving it of the necessary means to apply the rule of law.

It is also true of the community of states because there is still no world structure which is accepted as the embodiment of the force of law. The United Nations is a unique international democratic forum, but its authority has been weakened first by nearly half a century of the Cold War and then by unilateral actions taken by the major powers, in defiance of the very principles they profess to defend. The rule of law is indivisible; it must encompass freedom and welfare, individual countries and the world at large.

The Coming Water Crisis

Freshwater is emerging as one of the most critical natural resource issues facing humanity. The world's population is expanding rapidly. Yet there is no more freshwater on earth now than there was 2,000 years ago, when the population was less than 3 per cent of its current size.

Water is literally, the source of life on earth. The human body is 70 per cent water. People begin to feel thirst after a loss of only 1 per cent of bodily fluids and risk death if fluid loss nears 10 per cent Human beings can survive for only a few days without freshwater. Yet, in a growing number of places people are withdrawing water from rivers, lakes, and underground sources faster than they can be recharged—"unsustainably mining what was once a renewable resource," as one researcher puts it. Currently, 31 countries—mostly in Africa and the Near East—face water stress or water scarcity.

Population growth alone will push an estimated 17 more countries, with a projected population of 2.1 billion, into these water-short categories within the next 30 years. By the year 2025, 48 countries, with more than 2.8 billion people—35 per cent of the projected global population in 2025—will be affected by water stress or scarcity. Another nine countries, including China and Pakistan, will be approaching water stress.

Beyond the impact of population growth itself, the demand for freshwater has been rising in response to industrial development, increased reliance on irrigated agriculture, massive urbanization, and rising living standards. In this century, while world population has tripled, water withdrawals have increased by over six times. Since 1940 annual global water withdrawals have increased by an average of 2.5 per cent to 3 per cent a year compared with annual population growth of 1.5 per cent to 2 per cent. In developing countries over the past decade water withdrawals have been increasing by 4 per cent to 8 per cent a year.

Moreover, the supply of freshwater available to humanity is shrinking, in effect, because many freshwater resources have become increasingly polluted. In some countries lakes and rivers have become receptacles for a vile assortment of wastes, including untreated or partially treated municipal sewage, toxic industrial effluents, and harmful chemicals leached into surface and ground waters from agricultural activities.

Caught between finite and increasingly polluted water supplies on one hand and rapidly rising demand from population growth and development, on the other, many developing countries face uneasy choices. The lack of freshwater is likely to be one of the major factors limiting economic development in the decades to come.

Slowing Demand, Conserving Supplies

To avoid a water crisis, particularly in water-short countries with rapid population growth, it is vital to slow the growth in demand for water by managing the resource better, while at the same time showing population growth as soon as possible. Family planning programmes play an important role not only for individual reproductive health but also for sustainability of the use of freshwater and other natural resources in relation to population size.

As population grows, so does demand for freshwater for food production, household (municipal) consumption, and industrial uses. The availability of freshwater limits the number of people that an area can support and affects standards of living. In turn, population growth and density typically affect the availability and quality of water resources in an area, as people attempt to assure their water supply by digging wells, constructing reservoirs and dams, and diverting the flow of rivers. If needs consistently outpace available supplies, at some point overuse of water leads to the depletion of surface and groundwater resources, triggering chronic water shortages.

Scarce and unclean water supplies are critical public health problems in much of the world. Polluted water, water shortages, and unsanitary living conditions kill over 12 million people a year.

Competition for freshwater supplies breeds social and political tensions. River basins and other water bodies do not respect national borders. For example, one country's use of upstream water often subtracts from the supply available for use by downstream countries. As the 21st century dawns, there is a growing risk that wars will be fought over access to freshwater supplies.

If a crisis is to be averted, the world's overuse and misuse of freshwater must end as soon as possible. We cannot afford to keep wasting and fouling our precious supplies of freshwater. Increasingly, human activities are altering the flow of water and drawing down freshwater supplied faster than they can be replenished. Throughout the world enormous amounts of water are wasted due to inappropriate agricultural subsidies, inefficient irrigation systems, leaky municipal pipes, improper pricing of municipal water, poor watershed management, and other imprudent practices. It is time for widespread conservation measures, effective water management policies, and growing attention to assuring freshwater supplies and decent sanitation as part of development and public health projects.

Using Economics to Advantage

In the eyes of the public, the economic sectors—for instance energy, transport and agriculture—are often seen as pursuing interests that conflict with environment and health. They are the originators of pollution and often devise economic arguments to oppose changes in their practice that could improve environment and health. This behaviour has led the public, as well as environment and health professionals, to view economic analysis negatively. However, these economic arguments are often inadequate and unconvincing from the point of view of many economists.

In fact, the economic rationale is bound to reflect as closely as possible the preferences of the population and thus to take much greater account of environment and health. If used by environment and health authorities, economic analysis can be turned into a powerful tool for supporting their policies.

Why Use Economics?

First, economics can help to make explicit the benefits of environmental health improvements and the costs of the impacts. This provides additional arguments to encourage decision-makers to integrate environment and health considerations in their policies.

Second, current prices rarely reflect the full environment and health costs of the production or consumption of goods and services. Therefore, producers and customers have no economic reasons to reduce the impact they have on environment and health, as they do not pay prices that reflect this impact. Nor are they encouraged to take it into account in their investment decisions and lifestyle choices.

This could be corrected by reflecting as much as possible environment and health costs in the prices. Economic instruments such as environmental taxes or tradable permits are a promising solution. A first step in that direction is the removal of subsidies that support practices harmful to the environment and health. In most of the cases, however, it would be difficult to remove distortive subsidies immediately and charge the full amount of environment and health costs. Nevertheless, negotiating plans and timetable to do so progressively, is a strong signal to the economic actors. It modifies their anticipation of future prices, as they know they will have to pay in the future for the environment and health costs they will create. This drives them increasingly to design their long-term choices and strategies in an environment-friendly way. Finally, the setting of new economic instruments is usually under the responsibility of the Ministry of Finance. It also implies negotiations with economic sectors. Therefore environment and health authorities will need to play a more pro-active role in order to advance the integration of environmental health in sectoral and economic policies. Success will depend on their ability to discuss and present economic arguments in support of environmental health considerations.

A Promising Initiative

The present situation is that many environment and health authorities have few skills in using economic arguments and that economic sectors very often continue to ignore environment and health considerations.

International organizations—will also be invited to strengthen their co-operation in environment and health economics. In order to sustain the policy changes, promoting environment and health, co-operative efforts will aim:

- To support the development of the capacities of the environment and health authorities to use economic analysis;

- To improve the focus on health outcomes in national or inter-country processes dealing with environment and health issues. This will include the contribution of health expertise in these processes and the use of economic arguments to greater advantage;

- To exchange information early in the planning process of their respective programmes that use economic tools for addressing environment and health;

- To further co-ordinate their current and future activities in support of environment and health.

24

Law and Social Justice

Law reform in the service of democracy must find ways of protecting the vulnerable. Legal reform and "good governance" have vaulted to the top of the development agenda. International financial institutions and influential donors continually stress the importance of the rule of law, a healthy regulatory environment and strong and consistent enforcement of rights to successful economic development. In the new world order, the state's role is to facilitate private activity rather than guarantee the welfare of its citizens.

But there is growing concern that market reforms and globalization are connected to greater social stratification and economic inequality. What is often overlooked is that legal reform may enhance rather than alleviate this stratification and inequality.

It is important to see legal reform as a key part of a broader set of policy, legislative and institutional reforms which are designed to create not simply rule and norm-based societies but particular types of market economies. There are no "free" markets; functioning markets depend upon a legal infrastructure and a commitment to the rule of law. The growing interest in legal reform indicates nothing if not the widespread recognition of this fact.

Tradeoffs Between Efficiency and Equity

Respecting the rule of law and protecting rights however does not men that there is any one best set of laws, even in a market economy. Yet legal reform projects in developing and transitional countries have become inseparably associated with the idea of single, optimal path or model. Current projects emphasize strong protection for property rights, the consistent enforcement of contracts and, increasingly, financial sector regulation as the foundation of an investor-friendly legal infrastructure. At the same time, states in transition to markets have been discouraged from adopting or retaining "excessive" regulations, including protective labour market policies that might impede growth and efficiency.

Market-oriented legal reforms can affect the fortunes of different groups in at least three different ways. The first is through the types of reforms that are implemented. Because legal reforms allocate rights and entitlements, different rule structures may well benefit different groups in different ways. In some instances, there may be tradeoffs between efficiency and equity. Strong property rights will protect owners and entrepreneurs but may contribute to the disadvantage of renters and works; environmental and consumer protection laws protect the public at large but impose costs on businesses.

Second, people can be affected by the absence of particular laws. Labour standards and laws authorizing collective bargaining, for example, have been crucial in industrialized societies. If they are weak or missing as they are in many developing countries, or if they are indefinitely postponed because priority is given to implementing laws and regulations which facilitate economic transactions, vast numbers of people can find themselves worse off than they need be in the market for labour. Particular groups many also be harmed. Women with caregiving obligations are likely to be systematically disadvantaged and shut out of better work opportunities without market regulations which ensure that part of these costs are borne by others. This is especially likely where social programmes and subsidies are reduced or eliminated at the same time, as has occurred in many parts of the world.

Open Debate

Finally, where legal reforms follow a "standard form" or are designed by experts from after, a common experience in transitional states, the risk is that local history and priorities will be ignored or displaced and democratic control over decisions about basic social organization is weakened. To avoid aggravating inequality and worsening the position of those who are frequently already vulnerable in the reform process, three conditions need to be met.

First, conflicts of interests—between workers and entrepreneurs, for example—as well as the necessary tradeoffs that legal reforms often entail should be acknowledged openly, rather than hidden behind the veil of efficiency. This will allow countries to debate more openly the political and distributive choices that legal reforms involve. Second, donor countries and international financial institutions need to rethink the position that state "intervention" is usually or necessarily the enemy of economic development. Third, developing states need much more space, indeed they should be actively encouraged, to accommodate distributive, equity and social concerns not only through social programmes and transfers but through the processes of legal and regulatory reform as well. This would allow greater attention to labour market concerns and environmental protection as well as to poverty alleviation and gender, racial and ethnic equity.

AIDS and the Responsibility of the Media

HIV/AIDS is one of the most terrible diseases the world has ever known. Estimates are that 37 million people worldwide are already infected with the deadly virus which weakens the human immunity system and leaves the body unprotected for the onslaught of a host of other diseases. So far, there is no vaccine to shield people against HIV and there is no effective cure for the disease. This means that people inevitably die once they have caught the virus although same ten years or more may pass before the actual outbreak of AIDS in its final stages. UN figures say that 23 million of HIV/AIDS infected people live in sub-Saharan Africa alone—and all of them are doomed to die a painful death. At least 4 million newly infected were added to that number every year. As a result of the epidemic, life expectancy on the continent, which had been climbing persistently during the first three decades of post-independence development, will drop by ten years and more in many countries, especially in Southern Africa. And it will be the young economically active people—who are also the sexually most active ones—that will be prominent among the victims. AIDS thus is not only a humanitarian disaster, it is also threatening to become another source of economic retardation and backwardness.

Why then there is still so little attention paid to the looming crisis? Why are African leaders not getting together to discuss what needs to be done to control the situation? Why are they not using every means at their disposal to hammer the message home to their people: AIDS can be reigned in through more responsible behaviour and a change in sexual practices?

In Europe and America, when AIDS surfaced as a common threat in the late 1980s, every effort was made to alarm the public and especially the most vulnerable groups homosexuals, sex workers, people with frequently changing sex partners—about the dangers of unprotected sex. It was especially through the media that almost everybody became aware of the AIDS menace. Prominent individuals—film stars, pop musicians, artists—who had been infected with AIDS outed themselves in the media and used their fame in anti-AIDS campaigns. Existing taboos on sexual practices were deliberately broken, and safer sex became a publicly debated issue. Much emphasis was placed on using condoms as a cheap and simple, but usually effective means to avoid infection. As a result of the public awareness campaigns and the continuous media coverage, new HIV infections in industrial countries returned to a relatively low level, and the disease today is considered to be under control, even though no medical cure has yet been found to treat AIDS patients.

While these successes were achieved in developed countries, the disease has been spreading with increasing speed in Africa and, lately, in Asia. Here, the society has reacted with far less openness to the challenges posed by AIDS. For a long time, political leaders and the media negated the menace in the erroneous belief that AIDS was mainly a disease of the decadent West. When they woke up to the fact that AIDS was a problem not only for homosexuals in Los Angeles, London, or Berlin but also for "normal" hetero-sexual men and women in Uganda, South Africa or India, sexual taboos and religious inhibitions as well as social customs and attitudes proved powerful obstacles to launching publicity campaigns on the model of the Western countries.

As a result, there is still far too little information in developing countries on AIDS as a disease and what people can do to protect themselves against it. A recent study published by John Hopkins University in the United States, for instance, shows that only between 5 and 33 per cent of unmarried men are using condoms in sexual intercourse to avoid infection with AIDS. With women, condoms are even less known or popular than with men. The study says that the number of couples using condoms regularly is still very low worldwide. Instead of the 6 to 9 billion condoms used at present, 24 billion are required to control new infections. This is a question of money, because many of the people who ought to use condoms are among the poorest groups in breaking down barriers created out of prejudice and ingrained sexual behaviour.

Here, the media has a vital role to play. It is not enough to put up a few posters in town which warn against AIDS. The message has to be direct and concrete—Mechai in Thailand has shown how a witty and effective pro-condom campaign can be conducted even in a country with a strong Buddhist tradition—and it should not shy away from breaking sexual taboos. Equally important, all media should be used-newspapers, radio, TV. films, video—to carry the message. AIDS awareness should always be part of reproductive health information, and needed, both are part of the same coin: if more condoms are used to prevent unwanted pregnancies, a welcome side—effect will be a reduction in new HIV infections.

AIDS and the menace it poses to the survival of large parts of African and Asian populations is not a pleasant subject. But it will not go away by keeping silent about its threat. Political leaders and the media must make it a topic for urgent action And the people must change their sexual habits and behaviour and opt for safer sex. Otherwise, the future of whole regions on this globe will be grim.

Pollution for Export

After tax havens... pollution havens? are multinationals seeking to relocate in countries with low environmental standards? It all depends on how you look at it. In the search for new sources of capital, labour and raw materials are multinational corporations looking to relocate in "pollution havens" where environmental regulations are lax if not non-existent?

The question is increasingly being asked at a time when the level of foreign direct investment (FDI) is rising sharply. This is mainly due to fact that both "source" and "host" countries recognize that each has something to gain from the FDI process. However, some observers are afraid that economic gains are being generated at the expense of environmental quality and other important elements of social welfare. They worry that "host" countries will compete for the benefits of new FDI by lowering their environmental standards or by reducing efforts to enforce existing standards, and that firms will relocate to these "pollution havens", to gain a cost advantage over their competitors. In this scenario, developing countries are regarded as the most likely sites of pollution havens because they may be the countries most willing to trade off their environmental quality for economic gains, and industrialized countries are cast in the role of predators willing to degrade the environment of developing countries in order to generate economic gains for themselves. However, most research suggests that, overall, companies do not invest overseas to obtain access to lower environmental costs.

It is difficult to determine whether FDI flows are affected by the level of environmental regulations existing in foreign countries. Foreign capital clearly flows to a wide range of countries, industries and companies some of which are careful environmental stewards, some of which are not. A firm may in any case invest in a country to take advantage of a high quality labour force and other factors unrelated to environmental costs.

Respect for the Environment: A Good Selling Point

Environmental costs are often a relatively small component of total production costs, which may sometimes even be lower when environmental standards are higher (for example, where lower environmental standards lead to higher costs of treating industrial water supplies).

Multinationals often seem more interested in consistent enforcement of environmental rules than in lower standards per se. Moreover, companies are often willing to make new investments that actually improve the environment, so long as their main competitors are also required to do so. Part of the reason for this is that multinationals frequently apply a single environmental standard to their worldwide operations, regardless of any (lower) standards which may exist in a particular country. There could be three main reasons for this.

First, the firm may have calculated that it cannot afford to see the reputation of its products in the (global) marketplace tarnished by charges of "environmental exploitation" in one particular location—charges which can sometimes result in boycotts or other forms of consumer pressure. For example, investors in Puerto Rican banana production firms have insisted on "due environmental care" by those firms, because they perceive that overseas markets for their products will demand higher levels of environmental quality.

Second, the firm may have calculated that it is less expensive to apply a single environmental standard to its (globally integrated) production processes, rather than to develop 'tailor-made" production lines, based on varying levels of environmental standards.

Finally, the ability of firms to make " dirty" investments may be limited by requirements in their home country. For example, the US Ex-Im Bank requires any US company taking advantage of its export financing assistance to meet certain minimum environmental criteria.

On the other hand, there is some evidence to suggest that "pollution havens" do exist within certain types of firms, operating in specific industries, and in particular countries. Investments made in the resource extraction and processing sectors, such as chemicals, metallurgy, logging, and pulp and paper, fall into this category. In these industries, pollution control costs can make up a significant proportion of the firm's total costs. The result can be that small cost differences can translate into large changes in market share and profitability. These firms are more susceptible to the level of environmental costs, and therefore more likely to invest in "pollution havens". However, this does not necessarily mean that countries actually lower their environmental standards to attract new investments.

There is clearly competition, both within and between countries, to obtain access to new FDI. It is particularly keen in the rapidly-industrializing countries, and in countries which are dependent on the resource extraction and processing industries in which the potential for hard currency export earnings may be very high. In these situations, incoming investors can often successfully argue for relief from "high" environmental costs.

But surprising though it may seem, investors in resource-based industries do not always exert pressures for lower environmental standards—sometimes they may even want standards in the host country to be raised.

Competitive pressures can also translate into a desire to reduce waste and improve productivity, which can lead to improved environmental performance. An ethic of eco-efficiency, which seeks to "design out" pollution problems rather than deal with unwanted waste, is increasingly accepted.

FDI has also often associated with modern technologies which represent environmental improvements over what is currently available in the host country. Once the investment has been made, local firms may try to imitate multinationals' environmental practices. But there is also evidence that certain kinds of enterprises (e.g. the town and village enterprises of rural China) seem prone to use outdated technical equipment from other countries that does not represent the "best environmental technology", because they are undercapitalized and because this equipment is cheap.

There is also some evidence that "pollution havens" may be associated with something other than the level of environmental standards. For example, pollution intensities did appear to increase more rapidly in Latin America as a whole between 1970 and 1990, after environmental regulations in OECD countries became stricter. But it was not the countries with the lowest environmental standards which attracted the most pollution intensive investment it was those countries which were less open to FDI in the first place. "Pollution havens" were found, but they seemed to be more closely associated with protectionist economies than with lower environmental standards.

Overall, countries which operate straight-forward, transparent, and efficient environmental programmes seem to experience no particular loss of FDI flows, and may in fact attract some industries which are looking for reliable overseas bases of operation. In short, governments are recognizing that lowering environmental standards to attract new FDI is often unnecessary.

27

Human Rights–The Road to Progress and Peace

The UN Declaration on Human Rights has been fifty years old. A moment is needed to take stock and to look at the deficits which still exist in terms of human rights half a century later. The declaration of 1948 contains a comprehensive list of political, economic, social and cultural rights and aims at the protection of the freedom, equality, and human dignity of all human beings, irrespective of their race, gender, language or religion. Never before in history had there been such a far-reaching and solemn undertaking to protect each and every individual from all forms of oppression and deprivation. Two treaties adopted by the UN General Assembly in 1966 translate the ideas of the Human Rights Declaration into binding international law, and a High Commissioner for Human Rights, an office created as a result of the UN Human Rights Conference in Vienna in 1993, has been put in charge of monitoring the human rights situation and coordinate UN action on it. Numerous human rights NGOs all over the world, most important among them amnesty International, have established themselves as additional watchdogs to guard against human rights violations.

But inspite of all the attention human rights issues are receiving, especially in the western democracies, the progress achieved in guaranteeing fundamental human rights to every individual is anything but satisfactory. It is true: with the collapse of fascism and communism, and the disappearance of many of the military regimes in Latin America, Asia and Africa, some of the ugliest tyrants who trampled human rights under their feet have gone. Democratic structures are on the advance, and with them a certain measure of rule of law. In more and more countries, governments are elected by the people with means that they are to some extent accountable to their voters and cannot violate human rights with impunity. However, even where there is formal democracy and elections are periodically being held, social, economic or cultural rights are persistently denied to large groups of people.

In Africa millions of girls are circumcised (female genital mutilation) with grave consequences for their physical and psychological well-being—a serious violation of their human rights although defended by African males as cultural practice. In India, "the world's largest democracy", millions of dalits suffer from discrimination and exclusion because they do not belong to the caste system; tens of millions of children are forced to work under harsh conditions, ruining their health and missing opportunities for education; bonded labourers are toiling for rich landowners in rural areas; and girls and women are suppressed by customs which still grant all the economic power to men. There are good laws in India which forbid all these practices; but the laws are not enforced in the absence of strong institutions which reach down to the village level.

This is the situation in many countries: The existing legal framework guarantees the protection of human rights as enshrined in the UN Declaration. But the reality is quite different.

All these are accounts of the daily violations of human rights which are going on in many countries and which throw a long and dark shadow over the human rights. Most of those oppressed and stripped of their rights are poor people, those on the lowest range of the scale. Because they are poor, they find it almost impossible to assert their rights which they may hold under the constitution and the laws of the country in which they live. They are often illiterate and do not even know their rights, and when they do, they have no money to pay a lawyer and to go to court. For many of the more than 1 billion people living in object poverty, human rights therefore do not exist in reality. They are far from being able to live a life in dignity as demanded by the UN Declaration.

Human rights, therefore, cannot be protected in isolation from economic and social foctors. If we manage to reduce poverty, we will also help to improve the human rights situation. Development policy thus becomes a key to the problem without the enforcement of political human rights, social human rights cannot permanently be secured. On the other hand, the relisation of political human rights depends to a large extent on favourable economic, social and cultural conditions.

Human rights, when denied to people, can be a source of internal or internal conflict—just think of the millions of refugees who had to leave their homes due to ethnic and religious strife. The world would therefore be a safer place if full human rights were granted to all individuals in the world as proclaimed in the UN Declaration fifty years ago. Peace and progress would be the reward if we achieve this noble goal.

Energy

A Fair Deal for All

Both the supply of energy and the demand for it have spiralled in modern societies, where everyday life and changes to the environment, global as well as local, are conditioned by energy production and use. There is a crying need for a fairer share-out of material goods, energy and economic resources.

Energy comes in three forms: So-called "fossil" fuels (coal, oil and natural gas); nuclear power; and "renewable" energies (hydroelectric power, thermal or photovoltaic solar energy, wind an tide power, wood, etc.). Each of these has its own undeniable advantages and drawbacks.

Fossil Fuels

fossil fuels are abundant and very simple to use. Oil, for example, can be very easily transported and processed, and is relatively cheap. The technology for producing its many derivatives is highly developed. What's more, it is particularly will suited for use in all forms of land, sea and air transport. Its handy fluid form and its price make it appropriate to the needs of poor communities or those that are unable to invest in capital goods.

Fossil fuels account at present for 77 per cent of all the energy produced and will, according to the most realistic projections, still account for 73 per cent in 2020. The resources will be strictly limited geographically as well as in duration, being restricted to certain regions. This state of affairs is fraught with the risk of tensions and even conflicts, owing to the strategic importance of energy supplies.

Fossil fuels are furthermore responsible for the man-made increase in the carbon dioxide content of the earth's atmosphere, with the associated danger of an increase in the greenhouse effect and, as a direct result, global warming of the order of 1° to 4°C in the next twenty years, which would adversely affect the climate and the environment. Though much uncertainty remains as to the scale of the effects, the risk is great enough to mean that every effort should be made to slow down the increasing "carbonization" of the atmosphere due to the intensive use of fossil fuels.

Nuclear Power

The main advantage of muclear power is that it has no effect on the carbon dioxide content of the atmosphere. As it is also cheaper (per energy unit) than hydroelectric or thermal energy, some countries have opted strongly for this way of producing electricity.

Nuclear power is, however, far from being unanimously accepted. Public opinion is very conscious of the lack of candid information of the safety of nucler plants, two aspects that have not always been treated, in some countries, with all the necessary care and clarity by the authorities and the operators. The public is also worried about the disposal of long-lasting redioactive wastes, an acute problem to which the experts seem confident that a long-term solution can be found. It would also be a mistake to underestimate the danger of the spread of nuclear arms, even though the main powers are now significantly reducing their arsenals of these weapons. A final point is that only those countries which can afford to make the huge investments required can put nuclear plants into operation. The investment is offset by the low cost of the fuel but is recouped only in the medium and long term.

Renewable Energy Sources

The ecological movements, which are worried both by global warming and by the real or imagined dangers of nuclear power, would like renewable energy sources have to be developed faster than is now the case. These forms of energy at present supply some 18 per cent of total demand, which puts them well ahead of nuclear power.

Technology is moving rapidly forward in this field. These forms of energy are capable of meeting the needs of communities that it would be too expensive to connect to a central grid supply, but despite improved productivity and falling costs, they remain on the whole dearer than the two previous forms. It will be a long time before they can constitute the main source of supply. Other problems that remain to be solved include the major investments required for hydroelectric power stations and the environmental damage caused by the building of dams and wind farms.

We must face the fact that as of now there is no "miracle" energy that is risk-free for humans and their environment and is also cheap and inexhaustible. There is no such thing as absolute security as regards power generation and use, and it will not be possible in the future to do without any of the above-mentioned sources. Energy demand will continue to grow as a result of irreversible technological advances, of the justified demands of the non-industrialized countries, and of population growth that is in any case set to continue for at least the next fifty years.

Some Ethical Principles

A number of imperatives must thus be borne in mind by every individual, every nation and, in particular, the citizens of the industrialized countries. These are: the right of each individual to sufficient sources of energy; our responsibility towards our children and our children's children; protection of the environment; prevention of the potential major risks from the production of energy on a massive scale; the control of costs and the need to carry on with research in all these fields.

Some of these obligations—those relating to population growth, climate change or the disposal of nuclear wastes, for example—are of a very long-term nature, while others—efforts to deal with pollution caused by road transport or chemical waste disposal—are short-term. These differences of time-scale and the various possible interactions between the quantitative and qualitative aspects of the question have to be taken into account in observations of an ethical character such as the following:

- The present situation, whereby nearly one person in four in the world is without access to the energy resources he or she requires, cannot be accepted with resignation. Those with an active role in energy policy decision-makers, industrialists, research workers and so forth—must ultimately ensure that there exist, and continue to exist, sufficient resources of sufficiently cheap energy for the countries to have access to them, regardless of their geographical or economic situation.

- There should be no pretext for unnecessarily keeping the countries of the South, which urgently need proper infrestructures, on short commons as regards energy use. This is one are where, more than in any other, people need to be informed, so that they can take part in discussion and decision-making on subjects where scientific and technological knowledge is essential.

- Our duty to future generations enjoins us to use energy resources as sparingly and rationally as possible, especially as we know that a major part of these resources may be exhausted in a century or two.

- Even though rapid progress is being made in the exploration of space, we must acknowledge the obvious fact that we have only one Earth and must therefore preserve and protect it. Since energy production and use may jeopardize our environment, there is an urgent need for appropriate measures to be taken as rapidly and as effectively as possible. The management of nuclear waste and campaigns to combat all forms of pollution arising from energy use constitute unconditional obligations in this connection.

- Whenever massive quantities of nuclear or other forms of energy are produced or transported, e.g. when oil is transported by sea or big dams are built, major risks to life and health ensue. Absolute safety is unattainable, but the various energy authorities are nevertheless under an obligation to issue and enforce appropriate safety regulations.

- Unit cost will continue to be the main factor influencing the choice between different forms of energy. Production costs must be controlled and savings constantly sought if energy supplies are to be available to all.

- Research sometimes seems to have been neglected in work on energy production and consumption, but it is an indispensable duty. Efforts to find new sources of energy and more economical ways of using it must continue.

Food for the Billions

Will there be enough food to feed 8 billion people who will live on earth in 25 years' time? Surprisingly few people, at least in the industrial countries, seem to be overly concerned with this question. Whereas the world conferences on the environment, on women, human rights or social issues which were held in recent years were preceded and accompanied by intensive public debate, food does not seem to be a burning issue. Don't we have mountains of surplus food, people ask. Do we not have to pay our formers to leave their land idle in other not to add to the glut on the world markets? And hasn't the Green Revolution ended famine even in countries like India which used to be a synonym for hungry people? So where is the problem?

The advance made in agricultural production since beginning against a background of imminent crisis are indeed remarkable. In only 20 years, yields of major crops like rice, maize and wheat in developing countries went up by 80 per cent, outpacing even the rapid increase in population. But this growth in yields has slowed down in recent years, and the aim of "food for all" is one again becoming elusive. About 800 million people still do not have access to enough food to meet their basic daily needs, nearly 200 million children suffer from protein and energy deficiencies, 88 countries—44 of them in Afirca—have a deficit in food production.

Every one wants to increase food security. The definition is that "food be available at all times, that all persons have means of access to it, that it be nutritionally adequate in terms of quantity, quality and variety, and that it be acceptable within the given culture". To achieve this goal, more food must be produced—much more, because we must not only adequately feed the 5.8 billion people already on earth, but also the additional two billion who will be added to world population in the next 25 years. Critics argue that the problem is not one of production alone, but one of poverty elimination. People are not hungry because there is no food, but because they have no money to buy it, these critics say. Available resources must be better distributed to end hunger in the world.

However, even if we succeed to eliminate poverty in the next few decades—a feat which appears highly unlikely-there would still be the need to boost production, because with rising incomes people also want to eat more and better food including meat. As can already be observed in the countries of East Asia, the newly acquired wealth leads to higher consumption levels which puts additional strains on available resources are getting scarcer. Agricultural lands are being degraded at alarming speed by erosion, salinity, desertification or disappear altogether due to urban or infrastructure development. It has been estimated that 40 per cent of productive land now has diminished capacity to supply benefits to humanity due to direct human impacts of land use. Water for agricultural purposes is getting scarcer almost everywhere, and there are hardly any land reserves to be brought into production to widen the agricultural base.

In this situation, there is no alternative to increasing and improving production from the existing land area. This can only be done through research which finds the best varieties which will bring the highest yields at the lowest cost to the environment. Sustainable agriculture is the key notion—one that maintains bio-diversity, uses as little chemical inputs as possible and does not overexploit water and soil resources.

In recent years, agricultural research has been neglected—partly because of the erroneous belief that with mountains of meat and lakes of milk further production increases were not desirable. Since global grain production has stagnated and world stocks have reached an alarmingly low level last year there has been a noticeable change of mind. To raise the awareness among governments around the world that promotion of agriculture is urgent if hunger is to be avoided in the next century.

Important work is already being done by the international agricultural research institutes which promoted the Green Revolution in the sixties and seventies and are now again in the forefront of finding solutions to the daunting task of feeding 8 billion people by the year 2020. The International Rice Research Institute (IRRI) in the Philippines, the Maize and Wheat Research Institute (CIMMYT) in Mexico or institutes like ICARDA in Syria and ICRISAT in India which work on agriculture in semi-arid and dry areas, are all seeking solutions to the problem of raising production while at the same time preserving the environment. These institutions as well as national agricultural research institutions need all the support from the public and, of course, appropriate funding, to help them accomplish their task.

The scientists are optimistic that they can develop the varieties and farming systems which will allow mankind to feed everyone on earth well into the next century. But the task is not for the scientists alone. An economic and political order must also be in place which makes to possible to eradicate poverty and allow everyone to enjoy the benefits that science can offer. Feeding the billions is, therefore not only a scientific, but first and foremost a political.

30

Food Production

During the last 25 years, world agriculture successfully expanded food production faster than population growth. This can continue for the next 25 years and beyond, if appropriate action is taken. Although world food stocks are currently low and grain prices high, the world is not about to run out of food. We can produce enough food for future generations if we choose to do so.

The widespread food insecurity, unhealthy living conditions, and abject and absolute poverty in many developing countries are already threatening global stability. Failure to assure sustainable food security will foster the very conditions that will further destabilize and polarize the world in the years to come with tremendous consequences for all people.

The Basic Facts

Poverty is widespread in developing countries, with over 1.1 billion people living on a dollar a day or less per person. Human resource development in developing countries is lagging: 1 billion people lack access to health services, 1.3 billion do not have access to adequate sanitation systems, and one-third of primary school enrolls drop out by Grade 4. Natural resources, upon which future food production depends, are being degraded at alarming rates: almost 2 billion hectares of land have been degraded in the past 50 years: about 180 million hectares of forests have been converted to other uses during the 1980s, marine fisheries are collapsing around the world, and regional and seasonal water shortage afflict many developing countries. Improved appropriate technology is essential to increase productivity. Yet low-income food deficit developing countries are grossly underinvesting in agricultural research and many are reducing their support.

It calls for sustained action in six priority areas. First, we must selectively strengthen the capacity of developing country governments to perform appropriate functions such as establishing or clarifying property rights, promoting private-sector competition in agricultural markets, and maintaining appropriate macro economic environments. Predictability, transparency and continuity in policy making and enforcement must be pursued.

Investing in People

Second, we must invest more in poor people in order to enhance their productivity, health, and nutrition. It is not only unethical but economically wasteful that a large share of the world's population is malnourished, illiterate, sick, and without access to productive resources. Access to primary education, primary health care, reproductive care and family planning information, and clean water and sanitation must be assured for all people. Access by the poor to productive resources and remunerative employment must be improved. Empowerment of women must be supported.

Third, we must accelerate agricultural productivity. Agriculture is the lifeblood of the economy in low-income developing countries. In those countries, it provides up to three-quarters of all employment and half of all incomes. There are very strong links between agricultural productivity increases and broad-based economic growth in the rest of the economy. Agriculture is an engine of growth in low-income developing countries. National and international agricultural research systems must be mobilized to develop improved technologies focused on developing countries, and extension systems must be strengthened to disseminate the improved technologies and techniques. Low-income countries currently spend less than 0.5 per cent of the value of agricultural production on agricultural research compared to 2 per cent spent on agricultural research in middle and high income countries. An increase of agricultural research expenditures in low-income countries to at least 1 per cent of the value of a agricultural output is urgently needed, with a longer term target of 2 per cent. National agricultural research must be supported by a vibrant international agricultural research system that undertakes research with large international benefits applicable across boundaries. Current investments in international agricultural research are grossly inadequate to provide the support needed by developing countries. It is of critical importance that agricultural research result in reduced unit-costs of production. Such cost reductions will make food economically accessible to low-income consumers, and permit producer incomes to increase. To assure relevance of research and appropriate distribution of responsibilities, interactions between public sector agricultural research systems, farmers, private enterprises, and NGOs must be strengthened.

Fourth, we must assure sustainability in agricultural production and sound management of natural resources. Farmers, local communities, and governments must be encouraged to establish and enforce systems or rights to use and manage natural resources, to improve the way water is allocated and used, to reverse land degradation where it has occurred, to reduce the use of chemical pesticides and promote integrated pest management programmes, and to implement integrated soil fertility programmes in areas with low soil fertility. Local control over natural resources must be strengthened and local capacity for organisation and management improved. Investments in less-favoured geographical areas, that is, areas with agricultural potential, irregular rainfall patterns, and fragile soils must be expanded. Most poor people in developing countries reside in rural areas, and most rural poor reside in less-favoured areas. Yet, most investments, including agricultural research investments, still focus on the more-favoured areas. If we are serious about reducing poverty and protecting the natural resource base, the balance between the less-favoured and more-favoured areas must be redressed.

Fifth, we must reduce food marketing costs in low-income developing countries. The cost of bringing food from the producer to the consumer is very high in many of these countries. Efficient, effective, and low-cost agricultural markets must be developed in order to bring these costs down. Inefficient state-run firms in agricultural in-put markets must be phased out; investment in developing and maintaining infrastructure, especially in rural areas, must be forthcoming; policies and institutions that favour large-scale, capital-intensive market agents over small-scale, labour-intensive ones must be removed; development of small-scale credit and savings institutions must be facilitated; and technical assistance to create or strengthen small-scale, labour-intensive competitive rural enterprises must be provided.

Sixth, we must expand and realign international development assistance. Many years ago, industrialized countries had agreed to allocate at least 0.7 per cent of the gross national product (GNP) to international assistance. Most countries have not reached or do not maintain this target. Not only must the industrialized countries increase international development assistance to reach the 0.7 per cent target, but they must realign it to low-income developing countries. Also, contrary to the middle- and higher-income developing countries, the poorest countries are not able to gain access to capital from the rapidly expanding international commercial capital market. Developing countries in turn must seek measures to diversify sources of external funding, stem capital flight, and improve the effectiveness of the aid they receive.

31

Taking Poverty to Heart

Non-Communicable Diseases and the Poor

Non-Communicable Diseases (NCDs) are the leading cause of death worldwide. Their emergence as the predominant health problem in wealthy countries accompanied economic development. As a result, NCDs are often referred to as 'diseases of affluence'. But is this a misleading term? It suggests that these are not major problems for the world's poor, which is quite simply wrong, as this acticle illustrates. Is it time to rethink policy on NCDs?

NCDs include cardiovascular disease (CVD), such as stroke and heart attack, diabetes, chronic lung disease, cancer, diseases of bones and joints, and mental illness. The single biggest killer is coronary heart disease, followed by other CVDs, cancer and chronic lung disease. Diabetes is a major contributor to deaths from CVD, but also causes its own unique complications. Common risk factors for these conditions include smoking, physical activity, obesity and diets high in saturated fat and sodium and low in fruit and vegetables.

By 2020, NCDs will be the biggest cause of death in all regions apart from sub-Saharan Africa. It is predicted that in 2010, the number of people with diabetes worldwide will be double the level in 1995 and that the biggest increase (both proportionately and in absolute number) will be in poorer regions. CVD occurs at an earlier age in developing countries, increasing the potential adverse economic and social consequences.

NCD are already major health problems for adults in the poorest countries of the world. Demographic data show that age-specific death rates from NCDs in Tanzania are higher than in wealthier countries. Mortality rates for some NCDs, such as stroke, are particularly high. However, while NCDs account for 80 per cent of adult deaths in developed regions, the figure is less than 30 per cent in Tanzania, reflecting the continuing burden of infectious disease. Countries like Tanzania suffer the 'worst of both worlds'. Even within a country, 'diseases of affluence' is a misleading term. A more accurate label is 'diseases of Urbanisation'. Several studies from developing countries show increased levels of high blood pressure and other NCD risk factors in urban compared to rural populations. Even within urban areas, the more affluent do not always suffer the greatest burden.

The rise of NCDs in developing countries is inextricably linked to economic and cultural globalisation. This is exemplified by the activities of multinational tobacco companies. Tobacco-related deaths will exceed the tool due to HIV and become the single largest preventable cause of death by 2020. Curbing the effects of globalisation on the prevention and treatment of NCDs will also require regulation of food and agriculture multinationals and the pharmaceutical and healthcare industries.

Much of the projected rise in NCDs is preventable, particularly that due to smoking, poor diet, physical inactivity and obesity. Early action in some populations could prevent the emergence of these risk factors altogether; in others, the challenge is to reduce established levels. Although it is unclear whether all major risk factors are equally important in every region, the strength and consistency of data on the core risk factors in several ethnic groups justify preventive action now.

Lessons from risk factor intervention studies in rich and middle income countries suggest that success requires:

- Broad intersectoral action
- Community participation
- Appropriate legislation

- Involvement of appropriate NGOs
- Health Services changes—to manage those at high risk and promote public education.

Even apparently minor changes, such as a small fall in average population blood pressure, can have substantial benefits. However, some preventive programmes have produced disappointing results and almost all have failed to halt the ubiquitous increase in obesity. This highlights the difficulty of promoting healthy behaviour by individuals who are surrounded by barriers to change and inducements to lead an unhealthy lifestyle.

Health systems in developing countries face both a growing need for prevention programmes and increasing numbers of individuals requiring treatment. The complications of high blood pressure and diabetes can be reduced by the delivery of effective healthcare. Crucially, this entails:

- Partnership between patients and health professionals with the knowledge, ability and resources to take appropriate measures over many years
- Cheap and effective drugs and the implementation of simple treatment protocols, as promoted by WHO and the CVD initiative of the Global Forum for Health Research.

An appropriate policy and strategic framework is essential for such initiatives to be effective on a large scale. Even in the poorest countries people are already seeking healthcare for NCDs in both the public and private sectors, particularly in urban areas. Whatever the balance of priorities between different conditions, existing resources should be used as effectively as possible. Rapid evaluation methods can provide policy-makers with information on the current levels and equality of care and identify the main opportunities for improving health services.

The proper planning and co-ordination of NCD prevention and treatment, whether globally or nationally, requires up-to-date data on risk factor and disease levels—currently missing for much of the world. To address this lack, the WHO Non-Communicable Disease and Mental Health Surveillance section is promoting a standardised approach to enable comparisons across regions and over time, preparing the first ever 'world risk status' report for the major NCDs. This will provide a truly global perspective on the size and nature of the problem.

As this article has shown, NCDs are major health problems even in the world's poorest countries, including those regions where infectious diseases continue to take a huge toll. The NCD burden will grow substantially in low and middle-income countries over the next 10 to 20 years. NCDs will increasingly demand attention and require the right balance between competing priorities for prevention, cure and care. In meeting this challenge, national policy-makers will need to follow the lead of WHO and develop a strategic framework that plans for surveillance, prevention and appropriate health sector reforms.

Land Tunure

Securing Land for the Urban Poor

Around the world, especially in Asia and Africa, towns and cities are expanding rapidly, For the poorest people, finding affordable, safe and secure urban land for shelter has become increasingly difficult. This is because:

- Overall competition for land makes it increasingly costly;
- Central urban areas are being developed for commercial use;
- Natural features such as mountains or swamps limit physical urban expansion; and
- Meeting land management and planning standards (concerned with legality, technical and administrative accuracy) is expensive.

As a result, a large and increasing proportion of urban populations are forced to live in peripheral areas or occupy marginalised and dangerous locations. These settlements are often illegal and, providing inadequate shelter and lacking essential services, only exacerbate the problems of the poor. Higher levels of ill-health, unemployment and non-sustainable land-use often result. Furthermore, residents may also be under constant threat of eviction by government, and exploitation by landowners.

Experience shows that, if residents in such areas feel secure and safe from eviction, they do over time improve their neighbourhoods. Recognition of and granting of secure forms of tenure to previously illegal settlements often provides the incentive to communities to invest their resources in upgrading their housing and wider neighbourhoods. Security of tenure also brings the improved likelihood of basic infrastructure and other essential community services.

There is a wide range of urban land tenure systems. In many urban areas, including areas designated illegal by government, there are informal or customary tenure systems—these are often the commonest form the tenure and are expanding most rapidly.

While statutory or "legal" forms of tenure (for example freehold or leasehold agreements) offer many advantages, such as full individual rights and security and access to formal credit systems, they can also cause the very problems they were intended to solve:

- Higher rental levels, which may displace existing renters;
- The selling out of the secure land to higher income groups
- Encouragement of new illegal/informal settlements, as the poorest hope that they will also eventually get security of tenure;
- Encouragement of landowners and developers to hold land, without investing in its improvement or paying taxes on its icreased value—which serves to attract even greater levels of investment and land price inflation.

In addition, if people's incomes remain low and the capacity of the banks or credit unions is weak, statutory forms of tenure alone may not necessarily stimulate neighbourhood improvements.

Consequently, careful analysis of existing systems of informal and customary tenure and property rights is required, before embarking on major land management and tenure reforms. These can provide both acceptable levels of security and access to credit, which in turn stimulate improvements to local neighbourhoods. Before any decisions are made, tenure policies must recognise the likely impact on tenants, the poor and other vulnerable groups, especially women.

For these reasons, it is sometimes better to increase the rights of residents (e.g. by protecting them from the threat of forced evictions, or by increasing their access to essential utilities or credit), rather than assuming that they need freehold or leasehold titles.

Strategies for providing shelter now recognise the diverse nature of needs, and the positive contribution which decent housing makes to social and economic development at both national and local levels. They also recognise that the most effective way of mobilising the resources required is to encourage investment in housing by individuals, communities and the private sector.

Recent experience shows that many governments are now introducing positive approaches which are market-sensitive and encourage more efficient use of available land. These include measures to encourage landowners and developers to allocate a specified proportion of units to low-income groups out of profits generated from planning permission granted by (and therefore party created by) the government. Public-private partnerships and revisions to planning standards and administrative procedures have also demonstrated that it is possible to reduce the costs of access to land for the poor even under conditions of market-led development, thus reducing urban sprawl, the occurrence of slum settlements and levels of poverty.

Bibliography

Agrawal, Bina. 1992. "Gender Relations and Food Security: Coping with Seasonality, Drought and Famine in South Asia." In Lourdes Beneria and Shelly Feldman, eds. *Unequal Burden: Economic Crises, Persistent Poverty, and Women's Work.* Boulder, Colo.:Westview Press.

——.1997. "Bargaining and Gender Relations: Within and Beyond the Household." *Feminist Economics* 3(1):1-51.

Akerlof, George A., and Rachel E. Kranton. 1999. *Economics and Identity.* Washington, D.C.: Brookings Institute.

Alkire, Sabina. 1999. "Operationalizing Amartya Sen's Capability Approach to Human Development: A Framework for Identifying 'Valuable' Capabilities," Ph.D. Diss., Oxford University.

Baulch, Bob, 1996a. "Neglected Trade-Offs in Poverty Measurement." *IDS Bulletin* 27(1): 36-42.

——. 1996b. " The New Poverty Agenda: A Disputed Consensus." *IDS Bulletin* 27(1): 1-10.

Bebbington A., and T. Perreault. 1999. "Social Capital, Development and Access to Resources in Highland Ecuador." *Economic Geography.* October.

Beneria, Lourdes. 1989. "Gender and the Global Economy." In Arthur MacEwan and William Tabb, eds. *Instability and Change in the Global Economy.* New York: Monthly Review Press.

Berelson, Bernard. 1954. "Content Analysis." *Handbook of Social Psychology.* Vol. 1. Reading, Mass.: Addision-Wesley.

Bhatt, Mihir. 1999. "Natural Disasters as National Shocks to the Poor and Development." Disaster Mitigation Institute, Ahmedabad, India.

Booth, David, Jeremy Holland, Jesko Hentschel, Peter Lanjouw, and Alicia Herbert. 1998. *Participation and Combined Methods in African Poverty Assessment: Renewing the Agenda.* Department for International Development (DFID), U.K.: Social Development Division and Africa Division.

Bradley, Christine. 1994. "Why Male Violence against Women is a Development Issue: Reflections from Papua New Guinea." In Miranda Davies, ed. *Women and Violence: Realities and Responses, Worldwide*. London: Zed Books.

Brunetti, Aymo, Gregory Kisunko, and Beatrice Weder. 1997. "Institutions in Transition: Reliability of Rules and Economic Performance in Former Socialist Countries." Policy Research Working Paper 1809, Washington, D.C.: World Bank.

Carvalho, Soniya, and Howard White. 1997, "Combining the Quantitative and Qualitative Approaches to Poverty Measurement and Analysis: The Practice and the Potential." Technical paper 366. Washington D.C.: World Bank.

Castellas, Manuel. 1997. *The Power of Identity*. Malden, Mass.: Blackwell Publishers.

Cernea, Michael 1979. "Entry Points for Sociological Knowledge in the Project Cycle." Agricultural and Rural Development Department. Washington, D.C.: World Bank.

——, ed. 1985 *Putting People First*. New York: Oxford University Press.

Carnea, Michael, with the assistance of April Adams. 1994. "Sociology Anthropology and Development: An Annotated Bibliography of World Bank Publications 1975-1993." Environmentally and Sustainable Development Studies and Monograph Series 3. Washington, D.C.: World Bank.

Cernea, Michael, and Ayse Kudat. 1997. "Social Assessments for Better Development: Case Studies in Russia and Central Asia." Environmentally Sustainable Development Studies and Monograph Series 16. Washington, D.C.: World Bank.

Chambers, Robert. 1989. "Editorial Introduction: Vulnerability, Coping and Policy." IDS *Bulletin* 20:1.

——.1994. "The Origins and Practice of Participatory Rural Appraisal.: *World Development* 22 (7). Washington, D.C.: World Bank.

——.1997. "Whose Reality Counts?: Putting the First Last." London: Intermediate Technology Publications.

Chambliss, William J. 1999. *Power, Politics, and Crime*. Boulder, Colo.: Westview Press.

Charmes, Jacques. 1998. "Informal Sector, Poverty and Gender: A Review of Empirical Evidence." Contributed paper for *World Development Report* 2000. Washington, D.C.: World Bank. October.

Dahle, Cheryl. 1999. "Social Justice—Alan Khazei and Vanessa Kirsch." Fast Company, Issue 30, December 1999, www.fastcompany.com.

Dasgupta, Partha, and Ismail Serageldin. 1999. *Social Capital: A Multifaceted Perspective,* Washington, D.C.: World Bank.

Davies, Miranda, ed. 1994. *Women and Violence: Realities and Responses Worldwide.* London: Zed Books.

Dollar, David, and Roberta Gatti.1995. "Gender Inequality, Income, and Growth: Are Good Times Good for Women?" Policy Research Report on Gender and Development, No. 1. Washington, D.C.: World Bank.

Economist Intelligence Unit. 1997. *Armenia Country Profile, 1996-97.* London: The Economist Intelligence Unit, Ltd.

Edwards, Michael, and David Hulme, eds. 1992. *Making a Difference: NGOs and Development in a Changing World.* London: Earthscan Publications.

Edwards, Robert, and Michael W. Foley. 1997. "Social Capital and the Political Economy of Our Discontent." *American Behavioral Scientist,*40(5) : 669-78.

Esman, Milton J., and Norman Uphoff. 1984. *Local Organizations: Intermediaries in Rural Development.* Ithaca, N.Y.: Cornell University Press.

Fajnzylber, Pablo, David Lederman, and Norman Loayza. 1998. *What Causes Violent Crime?* Office of the Chief Economist, Latin America and the Caribbean Region. Washington, D.C.: World Bank.

Floro, Maria Sagrario. 1995. "Economic Restructuring, Gender and the Allocation of Time." *World Development* 23: 1913-29. Washington. D.C.: World Bank.

Folbre, Nancy. 1991. "Women on Their Own: Global Patterns of Female Headship." In Rita S. Galin, Anne Ferguson, and Janice Harper, eds. *The Women and International Development Annual.* Vol. 4. Boulder, Colo.: Westview Press.

Foley Michael W., and Robert Edwards. 1996. "The Paradox of Civil Society." *Journal of Democracy* 7 (3): 38-52.

Foster, James, and Amartya Sen. 1997. "On Economic Inequality after a Quarter Century." 2d ed. Oxford: Clarendon Press.

Fox, Jonathan. 1993. *The Politics of Food in Mexico: State Power and Social Mobilization.* Ithaca: Cornell University Press.

Galtung, Johan. 1994. *Human Rights in Another Key.* Cambridge, U.K., Polity Press.

Gelles, Richard J., and Murray Straus. 1988. *Intimate Violence.* New York: Simon and Schuster.

Giddens, Anthony. 1984. *The Constitution of Society.* Oxford: Blackwell.

Goetz, Anne Marie. 1998. "Women in Politics and Gender Equity on Policy: South Africa and Uganda." *Review of African Political Economy* 76: 241-62.

Greeley, Martin. 1994 "Measurement of Poverty and Poverty of Measurement." *IDS Bulletin 25* (2).

Grootaert, Christiaan. 1998. "Social Capital: The Missing Link?" Social Capital Initiative Working Paper No. 3. Social Development Family. Washington, D.C.: World Bank.

——. 1999. "Social Capital, Household Welfare, and Poverty in Indonesia." Policy Research Working Paper 2148. Social Development Family. Washington, D.C.: World Bank.

Grootaert, Christiaan, and Deepa Narayan. 1999. "Local Institutions, Poverty and Household Welfare in Bolivia." Social Development Family. Environmentally and Socially Sustainable Development Network. Washington, D.C.: World Bank.

Holland, Jeremy, and James Blackburn, eds. 1998. *Whose Voice? Participatory Research and Policy Change.* London: Intermediate Technology Publications.

Hyden, Goran. 1997. "Civil Society, Social Capital, and Development: Dissection of a Complex Discourse." *Studies in Comparative International Development* 32: 3-30.

Jackson, Cecile. 1996. "Rescuing Gender from the Poverty Trap." *World Development* 23: 489-504.

Jain, Devaki. 1996. "Panchayat Raj: Women Changing Governance." Gender in Development Programme. United Nations Development Programme, New York.

Kabeer, Naila. 1997. "Women, Wages and Intra-household Power Relations in Urban Bangladesh." *Development and Change* 28 (2): 261-302.

Kabeer, Naila, and Ramya Subrahmanian. 1996. *Institutions, Relations and Outcomes: Framework and Tools for Gender-aware Planning.* University of Sussex; U.K.: Institute of Development Studies.

Kaufmann, Georgia. 1997. "Watching the Developers: A Partial Ethnography." In R. D. Grillo and R. L. Stirrat, eds. *Discourses of Development: Anthropological Perspectives.* Oxford: Berg Press.

Korten, David C. 1990. *Getting to the 21st Century: Voluntary Action and the Global Agenda.* West Hartford, Conn.: Kumarian Press.

Krishna, Anirudh, and Norman Uphoff. 1999. "Mapping and Measuring Social Capital: A Conceptual and Empirical Study of Collective Action for Conserving and Developing Watersheds in Rajasthan, India." Social Capital Initiative Working Paper No. 13. Washington, D.C.: World Bank.

Krishna, Anirudh, Norman Uphoff, and Milton J. Esman (eds). 1997. *Reasons for Hope: Instructive Experiences in Rural Development.* West Hartford, Conn.: Kumarian Press.

Leach, Melissa, Robin Mearns, and Ian Scoones. 1997 *Community-Based Sustainable Development: Consensus or Conflict?* University of Sussex, U.K.: Institute of Development Studies.

Lipton, Michael, and Martin Ravallion. 1995. "Poverty and Policy." In Jere Richard Behrman and Thirukodikaval Nilakanta Srinivasan, eds. *Handbook of Development Economics.* Vol. 3. Amsterdam: Elsevier Press.

MacEwen Scott, Alison. 1995. "Informal Sector or Female Sector? Gender Bias in Urban Labor Market Models." In Diane Elson, ed., *Male Bias in the Development Process.* 2d ed. Manchester, U.K.: Manchester University Press.

Marshall, Gordon. 1994. *The Concise Oxford Dictionary of Sociology.* New York: Oxford University Press.

Max-Neef, Manfred. 1993. *Human Scale Development: Conception, Application, and Further Reflections.* London: Apex Press.

Milanovic, Branko. 1998. *Income, Inequality, and Poverty during the Transition from Planned to Market Economy.* Regional and Sectoral Studies. Washington, D.C.: World Bank.

Milimo, John T. 1995. "An Analysis of Qualitative Information on Agriculture: from Beneficiary Assessments, Participatory Poverty Assessments and Other Studies which used Qualitative Research Methods." Ministry of Agriculture, Food, and Fisheries. Lusaka, Zambia.

Moore, Mick, and James Putzel. "Thinking Strategically about Politics and Poverty." IDS Working Paper 101. University of Sussex, U.K.: Institute of Development Studies.

Moser, Caroline. 1998. *The Asset-Vulnerability Framework: Reassessing Urban Poverty Reduction Strategies.* Washington, D.C.: World Bank.

Moser, Caroline, Annika Tornqvist, and Bernice van Bronkhorst. 1998. "Mainstreaming Gender and Development in the World Bank: Progress and Recommendations." Washington, D.C.: World Bank.

Narayan, Deepa. 1999. "Bonds and Bridges: Social Capital and Poverty." Policy Research Working Paper 2167. Policy Research Department. Washington, D.C.: World Bank.

Narayan, Deepa, and Katrinka Ebbe. 1997. " Design of Social Funds: Participation, Demand Orientation, and Local Organizational Capacity." Discussion Paper no. 375. Washington, D.C.: World Bank.

Narayan, Deepa, and Lant Pritchett. 1999. "Cents and Sociability: Household Income and Social Capital in Rural Tanzania." *Economic Development and Cultural Change* (47) 4: 871-8.

Narayan, Deepa, and Lyra Srinivasan. 1994. *Participatory Development Tool Kit: Training Materials for Agencies and Communities.* Washington, D.C.: World Bank.

Narayan, Deepa, and Michael Cassidy. 1999. "A Dimensional Approach to Measuring Social Capital: Development and Validation of a Social Capital Inventory." Draft. Washington. D.C.: World Bank.

Narayan, Deepa, and Talat Shah. 2000. *Gender Inequity, Poverty, and Social Capital.* Policy Research Report on Gender Development, Working Paper Series. Washington, D.C.: World Bank.

North, Douglas. 1990. "Institutions and their Consequences for Economic Performance." In Karen Schweers Cook and Margaret Levi, eds. *The Limits of Rationality.* Chicago, Ill.: University of Chicago.

Norton Andy, and Thomas Stephens. 1995. "Participation in Poverty Assessments." Social Development Papers 9. Washington, D.C.: World Bank.

Orbach, Susie. 1999. "Psychoanalysis and Social Policy." Seminar paper presented to the World Bank, Washington, D.C., April.

Patton, Michael Quinn. 1990. *Qualitative Evaluation and Research Methods.* Newbury Park, Calif.: Sage Publications.

Portes, Alejandro. 1998. "Social Capital: Its Origins and Applications in Modern Sociology." *Annual Review of Sociology* 22: 1-24.

Pottier, Johan. 1997. "Towards an Ethnography of Participatory Appraisal and Research." In R. D. Grillo and R. L. Stirrat, eds. *Discourses of Development: Anthropological Perspectives.* Oxford, U.K.: Berg Press.

Putnam, Robert, Robert Leonardi, and Raffaella Y. Nanetti. 1993. *Making Democracy Work: Civic Traditions in Modern Italy.* Princeton, N.J.: Princeton University Press.

Ravallion, Martin. 1995. "China's Lagging Poor Areas." *American Economic Review, Papers and Procedures* 89: 301-5.

Ray, Raka, and Anna Kortweg. 1999. "Women's Movements in the Third World: Identity, Mobilization and Autonomy." *Annual Review of Sociology* 25: 47-71.

Rietbergen-McCracken, Jennifer and Deepa Narayan. 1998. "Participatory Tools and Techniques: A Resource Kit for Participation and Social Assessment." Social Policy and Resettlement Division, Environment Department. Washington, D.C.: World Bank.

Robb, Caroline. 1999. "Can the Poor Influence Poverty? Participatory Poverty Assessments in the Developing World." Washington, D.C.: World Bank.

Rodrik, Dani. 1998. "Globalization, Social Conflict and Economic Growth." *World Economy* 21 (1): 43-58.

Rupesinghe, Kumar, and Marcial Rubio. 1994 *The Culture of Violence.* New York: United Nations University Press.

Salmen, Lawrence. 1987. *Listen to the People.* New York: Oxford University Press.

——. 1995. "Participatory Poverty Assessment: Incorporating Poor People's Perspectives into Poverty Assessment Work." Social Development Paper No. 11. Washington, D.C.: World Bank.

——. 1998. "Toward a Listening Bank: A Review of Best Practies and the Efficacy of Beneficiary Assessment." Social Development Paper No. 23. Washington, D.C.: World Bank.

Sartori, Giovanni. 1997. "Understanding Pluralism." *Journal of Democracy* 8(4): 58-69.

Schuler, Sidney Ruth, Syed M. Hashemi, and Shamsul Huda Badal. 1998. "Men's Violence against Women in Rural Bangladesh:

Undermined or Exacerbated by Microcredit Programmes?" *Development in Practice* 8(2): 148-57.

Schwartz, S.H. 1994. "Are There Universal Aspects in the Structure and Contents of Human Values?" *Journal of Social Issues* 50(4): 19-45.

Sen, Amartya K. 1981. *Poverty and Famines.* Oxford: Clarendon Press.

——. 1983. "Poor, Relatively Speaking." *Oxford Economic Papers* 35: 153-69. Reprinted in *Resources, Values and Development.*

——1984. "Rights and Capabilities." In Amartya K. Sen, ed., *Resources, Values and Development.* Oxford, U.K.: Blackwell.

——. 1985. "A Sociological Approach to the Measurement of Poverty: A Reply to Professor Peter Townsend." *Oxford Economic Papers* 37: 669-76.

——. 1992. *Inequality Reexamined.* Cambridge, Mass: Harvard University Press.

——. 1993. "Economic Regress: Concepts and Features." *Proceedings of the World Bank Annual Conference on Development Economics,* 315-54.

——. 1997. *On Economic Inequality.* 2d ed. Oxford: Clarendon Press.

——. 1999. *Development as Freedom.* New York: Knopf Press.

Shah, Shekhar. 1999. "Coping with Natural Disasters: The 1998 Floods in Bangladesh." Seminar paper presented in June to the World Bank, Washington, D.C.

Shapiro, Gilbert, and John Markoff. 1997. "A Matter of Definition." In Carl W. Roberts, ed., *Text Analysis for the Social Sciences.* Mahwah, N.J. Lawrence Erlbaum Associates.

Silverman, David. 1993. *Interpreting Qualitative Data: Methods for Analyzing Talk, Text and Interaction.* Thousand Oaks, Calif.: Sage Publications.

Srinivas, Smita. 1999. *Social Protection for Women Workers in the Informal Economy.* Draft. Washington, D.C.: World Bank and Geneva: International Labour Office.

Standing, Guy. 1999. "Global Feminization through Flexible Labor: A Theme Revisited." *World Development* 3(27): 583-602.

Stone, P. J., D. C. Dunphy, M. S. Smith, and D. M. Ogilvie. 1966. *The General Inquirer: A Computer Approach to Content Analysis.* Cambridge: MIT Press.

Strauss, Anselm L. 1987. *Qualitative Analysis for Social Scientists.* New York: Combridge University Press.

Tarrow, Sidney. 1994. *Power in Movement: Social Movements, Collective Action and Politics.* Cambridge, U.K.: Cambridge University Press.

Tendler, Judith. 1997. *Good Government in the Tropics.* Baltimore, Md.: Johns Hopkins University Press.

Townsend, Peter. 1971. *The Concept of Poverty.* London: Heinemann Educational.

Tripp, Aili Mari. 1992. "The Impact of Crisis and Economic Reform on Women in Urban Tanzania." In Lourdes Beneria and Shelly Feldman, eds. *Unequal Burden: Economic Crises, Persistent Poverty, and Women's Work.* Boulder, Colo.: Westview Press.

Uphoff, Norman. 1986. *Local Institutional Development: An Analytical Sourcebook with Cases.* West Harford, Conn.: Kumarian Press.

Uphoff, Norman, Milton J. Esman, and Anirudh Krishna. 1997. *Reasons for Success: Learning from Instructive Experiences in Rural Development.* West Hartford, Conn.: Kumarian Press.

Visaria, Leela. 1999. "Violence against Women in India: Evidence from Rural Gujarat." In *Domestic Violence in India: A Summary Report of Three Studies.* Washington, D.C.: International Center for Research on Women.

Weber, Robert Philip. 1990. *Basic Content Analysis.* 2d ed. Newbury Park, Calif.: Sage Publications.

WHO (World Health Organization). 1997. *Violence against Women.* Geneva.

Woolcock, Michael. 1998. "Social Capital and Economic Development: Toward a Theoretical Synthesis and Policy Framework." *Theory and Society* 27(2): 151-208.

Woolcock, Michael, and Deepa Narayan. 2000. "Social Capital: Implications for Development Theory, Research, and Policy." *World Bank Research Observer* 15(2), Washington, D.C.: World Bank.

World bank. 1996a. *From Plan to Market: World Development Report 1996.* Washington, D.C.

——. 1996b. *Sourcebook on Participation.* Washington, D.C.

——. 1997a. *Poverty Assessment: A Process Review.* Operations Evaluation Department Document 15881. Washington, D.C.

——. 1997b. *World Development Report 1997: The State in a Changing World.* New York: Oxford University Press (for the World Bank).

——. 1998. *World Development Indicators.* Washington, D.C.

——. 1999. *World Development Indicators.* Washington, D.C.

——. 2000. *Poverty Trends and Voices of the Poor.* Poverty Reduction Group. Washington, D.C.

Wratten, Ellen. 1995. "Conceptualizing Urban Poverty." *Environment and Urbanization* 7: 11-36.

Index

A

Acid-throwing, 61

African charter on human and people's rights, 18

Agriculture, 77, 104

AIDS, 85-87

campaigns, 86

menace, 86

American Convention on Human Rights, 18

Annual Conference on New Development Finance, 68

Archaic attitudes, 14

B

Banking function, 64

Beijing conference, 43

Brazil, 69

C

Cardiovascular diseases (CVD), 107, 108

Changing gender roles, 2

China, 69, 76, 91

Clinton, Hilary, 68

Cold War, 75

Commercial microcredits, 63-70

alternatives to development bank promotion, 65

changing of development instruments, 63

downscaling or starting from scratch, 69

exclusion of small borrowers, 63-65

fall of the Berlin wall, 57

Conflict of interests, 84

Constitutional rights, 50

Control over their own bodies, 12

Controlled investment loan, 67

Convention on the elimination of all forms of discrimination against women, 18

Convention on the rights of the child, 18

Crisis of masculinity, 8

D

Decade of the Women (1976 to 1985), 48

Declaration of human rights, 18

Discrimination against women, 48

Discriminatory policies, 19

Divorcees, 50

Dowry deaths, 61

E

Earth Summit in Rio, 43

Education, 62

campaigns, 60

in Egypt, 11

their first struggle, 10-11

Elimination of poverty, 3

Empowering women, 6
Empowerment for women, 52-55
  integration to empowerment, 52
  lack of long-term strategy, 54-55
Empowerment, 2, 52
Energy, 95-99
  fossil fuels, 95-96
  nuclear power, 96
  renewable energy sources, 96-97
  some ethical principles, 97-99
Equality, 2, 3, 17
  and social justice, 8
  in a society, 61
  on all fronts, 31-35
Equation opportunities for women in the community, 36-38
  better opportunities to earn a living, 37
  changing minds in schools, 38
  equal pay, equal opportunities, 37
  getting women in positions of power, 37
  technological advanced, 36
  training to keep up with the times, 38
Equity, 2
Eradication of poverty, 43
Ethical character, 98
European Bank for Reconstruction and Development (EBRD), 69
– convention for the protection of human rights and fundamental freedoms, 18
Export financing assistance, 90

F

Family planning, 5
Favourably-priced foreign currency loans, 65
First female university was founded in Japan, 11
First International Women's Conference, 12
Food for the billions, 100-102
– production, 103
  basic facts, 103
  Investing in people, 104
Food security, 100
Foreign direct investment (FDI), 88, 90, 91
Fought for their rights, 10
Freshwater, 76, 77

G

Gender, 92
  based violence, 4-6
    social response, 6
    violence against women and girls, 4
  and Development (GAD), 7, 9
  ideology, 47
  is relational, 7-8
  training, 9
Gendered vulnerabilities, 8
Globalization, 74
Government's policy on international development, 2
Grameen Bank in Bangladesh, 66
Green Revolution, 100
Gross National Product (GNP), 106

H

Health care providers, 5
– facilities, 26
– workers, 6
Hidden promotion of exports, 64
HIV, 108
– infections, 87
Human Rights, 18, 20, 43, 74-75, 92-94

I

ICARDA, 102
ICRISAT, 102
Identities of men over life courses, 9
Ill-health, 111
Implementation of laws, 20
Impoverishment, 51
Incomes, 112
India, 69, 86
India's tradition-bounded society, 57
Institute for Cultural Action, 15
Inter-American Development Bank, 15
International organizations, 80
International Rice Research Institute (IRRI), 102
International Women's Year, 12
Invisibility of women in public life, 46

L

Labour standards, 83
Land tunure, 111-113
Language, 92
Law and social justice, 82-84
    open debate, 83
    tradeoffs between efficiency and equality, 82
– reform, 82
Librarian movement of 1968, 12
Lightening the load for women, 39-41
    breaking the poverty cycle, 39-40
    policy and research implications, 40-41
Living standards, 77

M

Maize and Wheat Research Institute (CIMMYT), 102
Market-oriented legal reforms, 83
Massive urbanization, 77
Maternal mortality, 25-26
Men and masculinities, 9
Microcredit programmes, 67
– Summit of 1997, 68
Micro-finance institutions (MFIs), 70
Midwifery skills, 26
Misogyny of the political class, 13
Multilateral institution, 53

N

New Development Finance, 68
NGOs, 9, 15, 28, 29, 30, 53, 66, 69, 70, 92, 105
Non-Communicable Diseases (NCDs), 107, 108, 109, 110
Non-sustainable land-use often results, 111

O

OECD countries, 91

P

Pakistan, 69, 76
Pollution for export, 88-91
    respect for the environment: A good selling point, 89
Poor nutrition and health, 57
Population Conference, 43
– growth and women's role in India, 56-60
    conventional wisdom, 56
    economic resources, 56
    female education, 57
    indifference towards women, 58
    nutrition and health, 58
    women and family income, 58
Population's impact, 71
    carrying capacity, 73
    ecological footprints of nations, 72-73
    environment resource accounting, 71-72

Position of women, 1
Poverty, 39, 56, 103
– to heart, 107-110
  Non-communicable diseases and the poor, 107
Professionalization on the NGOs, 53
Projectionist economies, 91
Promotion of women, 48-51
  global public for women, 48-50
  new opportunities, 50
Property rights, 50, 112
Protect children from the consequences of poverty, 39

Q

Quota, 29

R

Race, 92
Reconstruction Loan Corporate, 69
Redistribution of power, 50
Reduction in maternal mortality, 25
Reforms of law, 19
Relationships between men and women, 7
Religion, 92
Religious and youth groups, 9
Re-mapping the division between public and private life, 15
Rights of women, 3
Rights to vote, 11
Rio de Janeiro, 15

S

Safe motherhood, 18-24
  abortion, 23-24
  adolescents and children, 22
  barriers to access, 23
  delegation of authority, 23
  family planning, 22
  legislative and policy actions, 21
  regulation of practice, 23
  rights relating to
    equality and on discrimination, 19
    health care and the benefits of scientific progress, including health information and education, 19
    life, liberty and security of the person, 18
    the foundation of families and of family life, 18
Secular feminist movement, 61, 62
– society, 61-62
Self-help organizations, 50
Sex and gender, 1-4
Sexual taboos and religious inhibitions, 86
– violence, 6
Shelter, 113
Social developments, 49
South Africa, 86
Strategic gendered partnerships, 8-9
Sub-Saharan Africa, 85
System of information and customary, 112

T

Torture, 61
Trafficking, 61

U

UN Declaration, 93, 94
UN General Assembly in 1966, 92
UN Human Rights Conferences, 92
Underprivileged women, 35
Unemployment, 111
United Nations, 75
Universal Declaration of Human Rights in 1948, 13, 74
Untenable double burden, 16
US Ex-Im Bank, 90

USAID, 69
Using economics, 79-81
    promising initiative, 80

V

Victims of rape, 61
Violence against women, 5
Vision of democracy, 74

W

Water crisis, 76-78
    competition for freshwater, 78
    polluted water, 78
    river basins, 78
    scarce and unclean water, 78
    slowing demand, conserving supplies, 77-78
    water shortages, 78
WHO Non-Communicable Disease and Mental Health Surveillance, 110
Widows, 50
Wolfensohn, James, 68
Women
    additional sacrifices, 47
    and poverty, 42-44
    barriers, 27, 28
    decision-making, 35
    Development (WID), 7, 9
    education, 30
    electoral rolls, 30
    government's responsibilities, 44
    in authority
    lower-paid jobs, 46
    near absence, 45
    permanent commission, 30
    political parties, 30
    politics, 27-30
    professional employment, 45
    rights and obstacles, 46
    two types of obstacles, 46
Women's empowerment, 2
– human rights, 29
– lack of knowledge, 57
– organizations, 50
– organizations, 51
– poverty, 39, 42
– rise to power, 14
– struggle for their collective emancipation, 10
World Bank, 68
– – World Development Report of 1989, 65
World War II, 12
Worse off economically than men, 39

Y

Young girls' access to education, 59
Yunus, Muhammad, 66